RICH FOR GOOD

The How and Why of Wealth God's Way

BY JAMIE JONES

Tulsa, OK

Rich for Good: The How and Why of Wealth God's Way
ISBN 13: 9781680310993
Copyright © 2016 by Jamie Jones

Published by:
Harrison House Publishers
Tulsa, OK 74145

ENDORSEMENTS

Jamie Jones is a fresh, new voice sharing real-life, Biblical truths in a way that connects with readers of all ages — especially Millennials. In *Rich for Good*, Jamie tackles a hot topic that is essential for believers in the church today. Her heart is poured out onto every page with honesty and humor as she shares from her wealth of experience in a practical and fun-to-read way. I highly recommend Jamie Jones' new book because this book is a gift for those who desire to be *Rich for Good*!

Beth Jones
Author, Bible Basics Series
Pastor, Valley Family Church

Jamie Jones has captured the biblical principles of financial success in this very practical yet informative guide for anyone who is willing to submit to God's plan for their prosperity. Jamie gives real life examples of how these principles will work for anyone and how God honors His Word in our lives concerning our finances. I was both amused and educated in every chapter. This plan can and will work for anyone willing to be an obedient "doer" of God's word. It's a great read as well!

Michael James King, Attorney at Law
Winters & Kings, Inc.

DEDICATION

I dedicate this book to my family, Steven, Raleigh, and Ryder, my most beloved calling. Thank you for freeing me to follow the call of God on my life, even if it means eating grilled cheese, greek yogurt, or take-out on a regular basis. I am honored to serve God and reach the world with the gospel with you, and have fun while doing it.

FOREWORD

"The blessing of the Lord makes rich and he adds no sorrow with it."

Ephesians 10:22 (ESV)

In a spiritual climate where many are afraid to use the word "rich", Jamie confronts it head on with no apologies, as does the Word of God.

She takes this subject from the abstract to the concrete. There is no wondering, "what does this really mean?" By the time she has finished the thought, you know exactly what it means.

It's perhaps one of the most practical applications I've ever read on biblical prosperity, and I've been studying the subject for over 30 years.

When you finish this book, you will have the tools in your hands to make the same thing happen in your life that she's made happen in hers. I highly recommend it!

RayGene Wilson
Pastor, West Coast Life Church

CONTENTS

INTRODUCTION

To all of the people who said that money could never make me happy, you lied. In fact, there are few downsides to being rich. I have never wished away my wealth thinking life would be better if I could just struggle some financially. Honestly, besides exorbitant taxes and others feeling somewhat entitled to my money, there really isn't much negative about it at all. Actually, I would even go as far as to say that being rich punches being poor straight in the face. Sure, in a social setting, it would be extremely awkward if I just came out and told you how awesome being rich really is. (But it totally is.) When a bill comes in the mail, I pay it. Need a new car, I pick one. See a need that I feel like I should meet, I take care of it. Find something amazing to invest in, boom, I invest. So don't listen to those who try to steer you away from pursuing financial gain. Some may say it is greedy to want to be rich; I say there is no greed greater than not wanting to be. For if I am poor, I have nothing to give, but when I am rich, I can give to many.

I have been poor, and rest assured, being wealthy is definitely better. My husband and I have traveled from team poor to team rich hand in hand, and at times, even fist to fist. Our joint journey began with us being thousands of dollars in debt and living in Tulsa's tiniest third-floor apartment. Our spending was beyond our means, and honestly, we weren't even big spenders. As our pit seemed to sink deeper and deeper, the hope of financial freedom seemed to grow dimmer and dimmer. Having God as the foundation of our very lives, we had already surrendered this situation to Him, the way we did most everything. We had learned not to say, watch, or do certain things because we had made Him Lord. So if God was ruling each and every other segment of our life, this meant He must also be the foundation and ruler of our financial life. We became very aware that we needed God's miraculous grace as well as His clear directives to move us beyond our present pathetic condition. We were desperate for Him to intervene. We needed Him to impact the way we thought about money as well as the way we chose to use our money. We chose to invite Him to be the boss over everything we had, as well as everything we owed. Obviously, we weren't getting out of that pit on our own, or we would have already done it. God had to do what only He could do. At this time, however, our hearts were convicted that we had not been doing all that we needed to do. It was time to change.

It wasn't one big choice that shifted our lives. Consistently choosing God's ways is what caused the change. Some of the choices were very difficult; some were easier. However, we stubbornly chose to continue choosing His way. There was no particular or spectacular event in which we instantaneously reached financial breakthrough. Neither of us purchased holy water from the latest TV evangelist, which alas had set us free. Bless it. The truth is, there were just simple steps taken and simple choices made, consistently. That is it. How I wish it were one dramatic secret instruction that would instantaneously relieve your debts. What a lovely thought that we could one day muster all the gall to make one big choice and just be done with it. That is just not how God's way works, is it? He is a step-by-step, relational God. He prepares daily bread and morning-by-morning mercy. Each step of the way, God has whispered different scriptural truths in our hearts. This has been a literal pilgrimage in which we are still learning.

Rest assured, dear reader, we have not done everything right. You are in good company if you frequent 1 John 1:9. I am no perfect, prim and proper elitist; in fact, I am quite the contrary. Believe me when I say that I have missed it often! If you don't believe me, ask my husband, siblings, or even my kids. Jamie Jones knows no perfection. However, thank God, His blessings are not limited to my ability to do what is right all of the time. His blessings are limited only by His Word, which is also His way of doing things. So whenever you mess up, get up. It is all you can do. Maybe you are finding yourself in one crazy mess right now. You may have dug the pit so deep, there seems to be no way out. Well, my friend, it is time to pick yourself up, dust yourself off, and get back in the game.

I have taken God's directions, promptings, and leadings and crafted them into ten practices. I call them practices because they aren't instructions we received that we instatntly followed perfectly. They are practices because nobody gets it all right at first. We have to keep trying, stay focused, and not give up. Like a child learning to play t-ball for the first time, there are grueling moments to the process and a large learning curve.

Let's be honest, in t-ball there are painful moments. Moments when I want to yell, "The blast ball is on the blast tee! Hit the ball; it's not even moving!" Those first games are so difficult to watch. I speak from experience here folks; Ryder's first, and last up to this moment, t-ball season was circa 2015. Now, go with me to an Oklahoma June day, which can easily hit 100 degrees. Now imagine a plethora of four and five year old boys who would rather not be in polyester pants, longs socks, and belts in that heat. Additionally, add all of their highly opinionated parents sitting on metal bleachers with no shade (cause this makes sense, right?). There, the motionless ball that someone else had set up for them was, not moving, yet somehow, kid after kid *still* missed it. You guys, the ball was stationary. This was not fast pitch or even coach pitch; this was *no* pitch. There was no ball in motion, yet the little guys would still miss it. Why? They had never held a bat before, much less ever swung at a ball. They were attempting a motion completely foreign to their muscle memory. These particular muscles had never been twisted, turned, and released in that way. Their bodies had never bent and crouched in those positions. So they began to practice. They practiced swinging without a ball, without even a tee. The coach would have them swing in the air at nothing, just to have their muscles feel the motion of the swing.

Slowly, with the coach's help, the swings got better and better, smoother all the way around. Their swings became crisp. Before you knew it, they could swing and effortlessly make contact with the ball. Soon, the little guys would proudly walk up to the tee with chests bowed out, confidence evident on their cute little faces, because they had done this before. They would swing, hit, and run. The team I knew at the beginning of the season looked nothing like the team I saw at the end of the season. These were now more skilled kids. Kids who were formerly hopeless, you guys, but who now could play. You have no idea. My son used his glove as a Spiderman mask more than he used it to catch anything. How did these kids get from point A to point B? What made them grow into this team that was actually playing the game? One word: practice.

Practice can be defined as a repeated exercise in or performance of an activity or skill so as to acquire or maintain proficiency in it. All of us are on some level within our financial game. Some of us have never even seen a bat. Some of us have swung once, missed, and decided to give up. Others of us are stubbornly sitting in the dugout pouting because someone else hits the ball better than we do. The purpose of this book is to give you timeless practices to help improve your swing, whatever level your finance game is at.

Repeatedly practicing God's ways of handling your finances will eventually make you good at doing your finances God's way. You will become proficient in His system. Whatever you continually do will eventually become your habit.

Each of these practices is founded on solid biblical truths, which have stood the test of time. I firmly believe that if Steven and I instantly lost everything we have, if we were to keep true to these practices, we would be rich again in no time. This is no get rich quick scheme. This is simply a book of the ten practices God has given us that, over time, have made us financially wealthy. Although this book is written from my Western cultural vantage point, if we were to take these practices and drop them in a Haitian village in 1450 AD, they would have produced the equivilant blessings in that culture, for that era. How do I know? I know because the Word of God withstands all oppositions from all cultures and all eras. God never changes. His principles stand the test of time. His character doesn't change depending on what country we are in. Either He is for all of us, or He is not for any of us. Either He wants to bless all of His children, or He blesses none of His children. His truths have a cultural relevance for all peoples of all nations.

> **The counsel of the Lord stands forever, The plans of His heart to all generations.**
>
> **Psalm 33:11 (NKJV)**

> **Your eternal word, O Lord, stands firm in heaven. Your faithfulness extends to every generation, as enduring as the earth you created. Your regulations remain true to this day, for everything serves your plans.**
>
> **Psalm 119:89-91 (NLT)**

> **Jesus Christ is the same yesterday, today, and forever.**
>
> **Hebrews 13:8 (NLT)**

God's Word stands firm in heaven. You guys, if I may, in a society where nothing seems to ever stay the same, nobody seems to stay married, and change is a constant, this is very encouraging. His faithfulness has a reach that can touch all generations. Wherever you are, for whatever reason you picked up this book, you can trust that if you make these practices a part of your life, your economic situation will be better for it. Don't trust these practices because they have worked for us; trust these practices because they are rooted in the infallible Word of God.

"Jesus is the same yesterday, today, and forever." There is such security in these words. This is why we put our trust in God's ways. The stockmarket will change. Theories will adapt to culture. Supply and demand will consistantly be fluid. However, Jesus, never changes. What He has said is established forever. What a solid foundation we have been given on which to base our lives! Why would we not want to do exactly what the Word says concerning money? He is the everlasting God. From generation to generation, He remains.

This is what I want you to hear, right now, in this moment: You can do this. You can apply these principles and see change within your finances. You can learn from these principles. I promise you, we are nothing spectacular. We just listened, followed, failed, obeyed, and kept walking. You can too. I am excited for your journey! I believe in these practices so much, because they are straight out of the Bible. God wants to confirm His convenant with you, His child, so He is giving you the ability to get wealth. The pressure is not on you to attain success. It is God who will empower you; your job is to obey.

> **But you shall remember [with profound respect] the Lord your God, for it is He who is giving you power to make wealth, that He may confirm His covenant which He swore (solemnly promised) to your fathers, as it is this day.**
> **Deuteronomy 8:18 (AMP)**

Father, I pray that You would open the eyes of our understanding. Show us the right steps to take at the right time and the right ways. Correct our wrong thinking and teach us Your ways. Lord, we commit our finances and our ways of thinking about finances to You. Thank You for Your grace and wisdom. In Jesus' name, Amen.

THINK BIBLICALLY ABOUT MONEY

"Poverty isn't a money problem, it's a thinking problem."
— MARK HANKINS

Many people study successful people in order to become successful themselves. It has been said that becoming wealthy is less about knowing what a wealthy person does and more about learning to think the way a wealthy person thinks. If you can learn how the rich think, doing what the rich do becomes an instinctive, organic result. I believe that patterning your thinking after a wealthy person can prove to be profitable. However, as an even higher rule, patterning your thinking after what the Word of God says about finances will be even more profitable.

For just as the heavens are higher than the earth, so my ways are higher than your ways and my thoughts higher than your thoughts.

Isaiah 55:9 (NLT)

Renewing your mind to what the Word says about all things monetary creates a natural, profitable output of responses to life's situations. As our thinking is changed and renewed into God's thinking, decisions that used to be a struggle begin to process more naturally. We must take our thinking and submit it under the authority of the Word of God. Are our thought patterns about money in check with what the Word says about money? What about our habits? Do they yield to what Scripture says? This is the foundation of all of our practices.

> The fear of the Lord is the beginning of wisdom, and the knowledge of the Holy One is understanding.
>
> **Proverbs 9:10 (NKJV)**

Seeking Him and His thoughts and being yielded to His ways are the only true ways to attain wisdom. God WANTS to give you wisdom. He wants to impart His thoughts to you. As earthly parents long to impart what they know to their children, He longs to do the same for you. His wisdom will teach you how to truly reach your potential.

> Don't copy the behavior and customs of this world, but let God transform you into a new person by changing the way you think. Then you will learn to know God's will for you, which is good and pleasing and perfect.
>
> **Romans 12:2 (NLT)**

This scripture applies to every area of our lives. If we can align our thinking with God's Word, we will be changed. As we know His will, which comes from His Word, we can walk out steps that are good, pleasing, and perfect in His sight.

Thinking on, mediating on, and studying what the Word says about God's character and His attributes concerning finances is a must to becoming wealthy God's way. If you can get His mind on financial matters, your biblically guided choices concerning finances will begin to fuel His system. It is easy to yield to the world's way of doing things. I mean, come on; we come out of the womb with an attitude that the whole world should revolve around us, and we will cry louder and harder until it does. As soon as we can utter our first words, we let whoever is listening know that the toy in front of us is "Mine! Mine! Mine!" Copying the behavior of the world is easy and even feels natural. We don't have to try to be selfish. We just are. We don't have to try to want what we want and want it right now; we just do.

Although we may be born this way, we don't have to stay this way. By His Word, we can let our Father transform us into new people. His words become our words, His thoughts our thoughts, and before we know it, the process of what and how we think looks completely different than it used to. Not only does He transform our thoughts, but our very process of thinking becomes completely recalibrated. His Word has the ability to craft us into new people. The ugly, the selfish, the stink that only we know about, yielded to His system, can be forever changed. Only He can change us. We cannot do it through willpower and stamina. It isn't done by repeating the right words a certain number of times, with a certain holy inflection. A positive confession alone can turn the wheel, but it can not move the car. It is only by learning and leaping into His system that we are changed. This is where the mind-blowing power and breathtaking beauty of the perfect Word of God is revealed.

Our God is the One who literally spoke life into existence.

There was nothing. There was void, darkness, and a cascade of empty. Then He spoke, and light and life was. Light, which had never existed, shone. Life, which never was, breathed its first breath, and era after era, continues breathing. He is the One who created the tides, the oceans, and the beautiful depths within. Our Father formed man, crafted woman, and set in place a glorious system where we could reproduce His creative process and have fun doing it. To call Him a genius is the understatement of all time. He not only is the creator of all beings, but also the creator of systems. From the ecosystem to the solar system, His ways are beyond our thinking. He has established the heavens and the earth with authority and precision. This is the same God who has also created the world's best economic system.

This system is different than the Forbe's, CNN, or the Nasdaq's systems. In His system, we receive by giving, grow by pruning, and our greatness is defined by our serving. Although His ways are not our ways, He welcomes us to partake of His higher thinking. One thought, once choice, one yielded step at a time, we can join this rhythm. As our thoughts are taken captive and aligned with His Word, we jump into a system that was set in place long before the American dollar even existed.

The temptation we face is to shrink back into our own cultural thinking. It has a way of hauntingly creeping back in, one crooked, little bony finger at a time. A choice to be consistent must rise up as we continuously take hold of these thoughts and subject them to what the Bible has to say. In times of doubt, I talk to myself.

"Jamie Beth, do you really think you know a better way than His? I mean, He is the One who put the law of gravity into place to keep your little booty on this earth so it doesn't go flying into the great abyss. His ways are still higher. His thoughts are still wiser. So, flesh, shut it. I am going on with God."

We must be alert and careful, lest we sleepily slip into our old ways of earthly systematic thinking. We can either pattern our choices on what is culturally relevant, or we can let the Bible become our guide and standard. This is how my husband and I accumulated and adapted these practices. We hung the way we thought by purposefully yielding to the Word of God as our authority on finances. Sometimes (possibly all the time, all the days, all the minutes), it goes against our nature to yield to what the Word says, especially concerning money. In the times when we absolutely do not want to do what we know is right, we must remind ourselves of the most elementary truth: God is smarter than we are.

I realize this is the most obvious of statements. Of course, He is smarter. One of us created the universe; one of us didn't. One of us is smarter than each and every neuroscientist on the planet; one of us is not. One of us knows the genetic make-up of the world's most complicated species; one of us forgets where she places her keys on a daily basis. When you really begin to think how ridiculous it is to choose a way other than God's way, it is in fact, quite humorous. Why do we do this all of the time? Do you base your financial decisions on the fact that it is more blessed to give than to receive? Do you know and trust that God wants you to prosper? Do you trust that He provides seed to the sower?

If you don't know that I am originally from Texas, just talk to me for five minutes, and somehow, I will make sure you know. I am a lover of all things Texas from the BBQ, to the beautiful rivers, to the friendly culture, to the lonely cow-lined highways. I went to high school in one of the most beautiful towns Texas has to offer, New Braunfels. New Braunfels is a German settlement with many unique, quaint attributes. Most Texans know of my beloved New Braunfels because of Schlitterbahn, the country's most attended seasonal waterpark. Schlitterbahn is like the Disney World of summer water fun, aka, "the hottest, coolest time in Texas." One of my favorite features is the Krystal River at the Surfenberg location. This is a traditional lazy river that has a calm and steady pace as it transports you around the circumference of the whole park. I have loved this ride since I was a teenager because of the hidden torrential current bursts. See, if you know right where to go, and you're willing to wait for the timing of their automatic circulating system, you can jump in and be swept away on this thrilling invisible current. A rush of water lets out in this one particular spot and if you know when and where to hop in, you hit the current and are whisked away at a thrilling speed. It just takes a little effort from me, and I am zooming past everyone else. Try as they might in all of their efforts, tube or no tube, running or arms flailing, I can still beat them. Why? I am yielded to the system already set in place. I do my part to jump in, and I trust the timing. The rest is up to the system.

Through the years, I have seen so many striving to attain a certain financial status. Whether it's the latest multi-level marketing product, the latest "You too can be awesome!" seminar, or people tirelessly spinning themselves dizzy on their own busy wheels, they never reach their goals. They become defeated and end up in a spiraling state of exhaustion. These things are not all bad, but they are meant to be a supplement to God's system, not replace the system itself. You see, when we trust God's timing and jump into His way of doing things, we get to ride on His current. Just like at Schlitterbahn, you fit into the system that has already been created. You replace exhausting striving for refreshing yielding. God's ways of doing things can expedite you farther faster than your own efforts ever could.

At the level you are convinced God's ways are best is the same level you will value learning His kingdom's thinking. Can you see yourself riding in the current of His kingdom? Can you see yourself valuing giving more than receiving? Can you see yourself trusting His timing while you plant the seeds you have in your hands? Can you see yourself being propelled past the level striving would reached?

The Bible has over two thousand scriptures about money. Seems to me that the Lord would really like to get something across to us concerning our finances. Engulfing yourself in biblical, financial thinking, transforms your thought patterns.

Here are a few scriptures straight out of the the Bible on finances. To really absorb His system, we must take time to know it. I challenge you not to rush to the next chapter but to soak in His words for a few moments. Take the time to pause and read them and write them down on a notecard or in a notebook. Do one or two of these verses really stick out to you? Do they seem to be highlighted in your heart? Put them in your car, on your mirror, by your nightstand, or on your computer. Remember, we have a whole system to learn, so we must surround ourselves in this way of thinking. It is so worth you taking time to slow down in order to write down these scriptures. The time invested in learning God's monetary culture will always bring profitable dividends.

Take a moment to look at these verses, and see what the Bible says about your finances:

And my God will supply all your needs according to His riches in glory by Christ Jesus.

Philippians 4:19 (NKJV)

According to Philippians 4:19, as believers, who supplies our needs?

And God is able to make every grace overflow to you, so that in every way, always having everything you need, you may excel in every good work.

2 Corinthians 9:8 (HCBS)

According to 2 Corinthians 9:8, how often should we have our needs met?

I walk in the way of righteousness, along the paths of justice, giving wealth as an inheritance to those who love me, and filling their treasuries.

Proverbs 8:20-21 (HCBS)

According to Proverbs 8:20 and 21, does God want to add to our monetary status or take from it?

Give, and it will be given to you. A good measure, pressed down, shaken together, and running over, will be poured into your lap. For with the measure you use, it will be measured back to you.

Luke 6:38 (NIV)

From its description in Luke 6:38, how is God's system different from the world's?

"Bring the whole tithe into the storehouse, that there may be food in my house. Test me in this," says the LORD Almighty, "and see if I will not throw open the floodgates of heaven and pour out so much blessing that there will not be room enough to store it."

Malachi 3:10 (HCSB)

Honor the LORD with your possessions and with the first produce of your entire harvest; then your barns will be completely filled, and your vats will overflow with new wine.

Proverbs 3:9-10 (HCSB)

In both of these scriptures, who initiates the process of giving?

You have to be completely settled in your heart that God wants you to have money and that He wants you to give money. Renewing your mind is possibly more than half the battle.

God, open our eyes that we may understand Your system. Help us to think Biblically about money. Lord, I ask that You would lead us to scriptures that would strengthen our belief system. Thank you Lord for teaching me. Amen.

SOW AT ALL TIMES: BOTH REFLEXIVELY AND INTENTIONALLY

"The first and foremost benefit to wealth in our opinion, is to be thoroughly equipped for every good work."
– RUSTY AND KIM HUTSON

The financial arena is very similar to a garden. What we put into it is exactly what we get out of it. When you first plant, it is difficult to imagine a tiny, seemingly insignificant seed will one day produce a full meal.

In my last garden, I planted cucumbers, tomatoes, onions, watermelon, kale, cantaloupe, and of course, jalapeños. (Did I mention I am from Texas? We practically put jalapeños in our baby's bottles.) Before planting, I held the seeds in my hand. I could feel them and see them. Then the time came for me to create a tiny hole in the soil, place the seed in the hole, and cover the seed with dirt. My hands were now empty, void of my seeds. The dirt looked barren and smooth. However, it wasn't hard for me to do this. I wasn't sad to let go of the seed. My focus wasn't on my empty hand. Why? Because I knew the seeds kept within my hand held nothing but potential. However, the seeds in the correct environment would be crafted into a beautiful harvest. Seeds were planted, but a family meal would be yielded. While carefully covering up the tiny watermelon seed, no tear was shed, rather, I had hope of what would evolve after time—a ripe, gorgeous, juicy watermelon!

Sometimes, giving money can seem far less happy and hopeful. To be honest, I can think of times when giving seemed almost physically painful. It was as if part of us, our future, our dreams, were just hiding in the dirt, possibly never to be seen again. Looking back, I can now see that part of us didn't trust the system that God had established. Our faith needed to grow in this area. We needed to be fully persuaded in what the Word of God said in this area. We reap what we sow. It is straight Bible, y'all. You plant good; you grow good. You plant bad; you grow bad. You plant nothing; you grow nothing.

Can I suggest that we quit viewing giving as a painful sacrifice and instead see it as a prosperous process that helps? Each seed planted is an opportunity for God to cause growth in our lives. Until we fully trust His system by renewing our minds to what His Word says, we must grit our teeth, dig our heels in the sand, and resist the opportunity to feel like we are throwing money away and not sowing it away. Sowing money away is much different than throwing it away. Sowing money away is a temporary release of control, which allows God to multiply what was once yours.

Now this I say, he who sows sparingly will also reap sparingly, and he who sows bountifully will also reap bountifully.

Each one must do just as he has purposed in his heart, not grudgingly or under compulsion, for God loves a cheerful giver. And God is able to make all grace abound to you, so that always having all sufficiency in everything, you may have an abundance for every good deed; as it is written,
"HE SCATTERED ABROAD, HE GAVE TO THE POOR, HIS RIGHTEOUSNESS ENDURES FOREVER."
Now He who supplies seed to the sower and bread for food will supply and multiply your seed for sowing and increase the harvest of your righteousness; you will be enriched in everything for all liberality, which through us is producing thanksgiving to God.

2 Corinthians 9:6-11 (NASB)

Do you see how much our hearts are emphasized? God doesn't want your money; He wants your heart. Money is never lacking for Him. He can make a coin appear in a fish's mouth if necessary. Throughout the gospels, Jesus is always focused on our hearts.

And He looked up and saw the rich putting their gifts into the treasury. And He saw a poor widow putting in two small copper coins. And He said, "Truly I say to you, this poor widow put in more than all of them; for they all out of their surplus put into the offering; but she out of her poverty put in all that she had to live on."

Luke 21:1-4 (NASB)

The widow gave all she had to live on. Don't you know that this pleased the Father? She trusted Him to meet her needs as she was longing to meet the needs of others. I love that she didn't see her seed as too insignificant. Her two copper coins were more valuable to Him than the large amounts the rich gave out of their surplus. Her two coins represented a whole heart while their extra money represented a heart unyielded.

God loves a cheerful giver! A cheerful giver is someone who is happy to plant seed into God's system. Being a cheerful giver means that you trust Him. You also trust His words. It means that you know you will reap bountifully. You will never lack by giving. The Word says that in the same measure you give, you will reap. When you know this, you are glad to give! You are able to help the church, the hungry, the poor, and others; at the same time, you get a full return. Through the process of sowing and reaping, God is trying to get more to you, not more out of you.

God will multiply what we give to Him and enrich us. We will be able to give to every good work. Isn't that amazing? God wants His children on the side of meeting needs. He wants you to be His vessel to help the poor, feed the hungry, clothe the naked, and house the orphan. It truly is more blessed to give than to receive.

This past Christmas, our church was doing an outreach for the underprivileged within our own city. I approached the outreach table expecting to buy a few toys for these families. The needs were overwhelming. These kids weren't just needing a present to open on Christmas morning. These children were needing basic necessities, which my kids have never had to even think about. Due to the lack in these families, some of the children were in danger of being removed from their homes. CPS was not removing these children because there was abuse, but because basic physical needs couldn't be met. The Holy Spirit grabbed ahold of my heart and pointed out a specific need to me. I could barely fight back tears as I asked the lady how many kids needed this. I was in disbelief that in our own city, precious children needed such basic essentials. I grabbed all of the cards with that specific need and told my husband I wanted to take care of all of them. Without flinching, he agreed; we *had* to do this. The joy that rose up in our hearts was indescribable. We were so honored that God led us straight to these needs and used us to touch the most precious of His creation, children. The freedom to give is a sobering privilege. I am able to help others. In return, God helps me and mine. The deposit that He places in our hearts when we give is much greater than the withdrawal we take from our bank account.

What good is a seed if it forever remains a seed? This is in every area, not just the financial realm. If we sow effort into our relationship with God, we are strengthened and grow spiritually. If we invest time in our relationships, they grow. If we work out, and invest into our physical body, we will reap a healthier body. The value of a seed is within it's ability to grow, not to remain.

One of the practices we have is to always be sowing something. In return, this means we will always be harvesting something. In gardening, there are some vegetables like beans and onions, that gardening experts suggest you plant every three to four weeks. By doing this, you have a constant, steady growth of your veggies. Steven and I try to plant a few things each and every day. We rush to be the ones who buy the coffee for our friends, sneak the ticket from the server to pay for dinner, pay for groceries for the person behind us, and anything else we can think of! What fun is it to slip a cute bracelet off of my wrist onto the unsuspecting wrist of my friend? These seeds may not change the world by themselves, but they are feeding a biblical system that will produce more seeds. More seeds will, in fact, change the world. These small, seemingly insignificant seeds are always coming up bigger and better, providing more seeds than before. A constant flow into the system will eventually produce a constant flow out.

Sowing constant seed has multiple benefits. Feeding your account is just one of them. The second is that your position will be shifted from being a need seeker to a need meeter. Now you will be privileged to be an answer to someone else's prayer. Is this not the heart of God, that we look to serve each other instead of solely serving ourselves? A heart to serve others is the polar opposite of our current narcissistic world. I have found a good thermometer of this is to ask yourself, "What am I praying for?" Are your prayers solely focused on what you are lacking? Is the majority of your energy aimed at what you need and want? Or are your prayers focused on asking God to send you someone who has a need that you can meet?

This is something you can teach your children as well. In today's society, children are being taught that the world revolves around them. This selfish, wrong thinking is bound to produce egotistical, narcissistic adults who do not know the beauty of giving. My kids don't go to school with a bag of money looking for someone with a need to bless. However, they do have friendship and love that they can give freely. Every morning we pray, "Lord, send us someone we can love on today to help make his or her day brighter. Open a door for us to show someone how good You are and how much You love them." This is an intentional act on my part to shift my children's mindset first thing in the day. Imagine what the body of Christ would be like in the next generation if we all did this.

We would be raising up leaders who are focused on other people's needs and praying that God would use them to do so. I don't care if you are nostril-high in debt, you have something that you can give to someone. Maybe you can give hope, a hug, or an hour of free babysitting. Never negate the size of a seed.

Whenever we are focused on helping others, God knows that we are not attached to our stuff and that we will freely share what He has provided. There is such life in being a conduit of His goodness. You can start this right now, wherever you are, whoever you are, and whatever your financial standing is. Think about what the church would look like, if this were our aim. What if we took the law of sowing and reaping and made it literal in our lives? I want you to take an honest evaluation of your own life's garden right now. Imagine a plot of dirt about ten by ten feet. In this dirt are all of the seeds you have sown. Are there seeds sprouting in your garden? Are the sprouts growing good things? Are there seeds that you have been planting that aren't coming up yet? Do you have hope that they will? What about a harvest? Do you have any fully mature fruit? Have weeds of doubt tried to choke some of your harvest? What does your garden look like?

Take a moment and imagine yourself planting more seeds. Think of the different seeds you could begin sowing today. Maybe you can't buy a single mother a car right now, but could you buy someone coffee? Maybe you can't even buy your own coffee. Could you mow your neighbor's lawn?

I know someone out there may be reading this thinking you literally have nothing to give. Believe me, I totally understand. I really can relate. I get it. I was so that person. I have many stories of God's faithfulness in taking a seed and producing a harvest. There have been countless moments where it looked like I was not going to make it, like at all. Then God came through! As a young adult, I attended two different Bible colleges, one in Oklahoma and one in Texas. Yes people, I was a professional Bible school student. While I was in Oklahoma, although I had a job, I was mainly living on my parents' dime. When I left for Texas, that pretty little well ran dry. My parents were pioneering a church at that time, and they had no money to spare. I had gone from having a dad who worked in the oil industry to a dad who was scraping by in order to help his church.

This was a complete financial culture shock for me. From childhood, I remember the most amazing display of presents on any given Christmas. They would tower up next to the Christmas tree, taking up much of the living room floor. Since money had now grown tight, there were Christmases when my sweet mom would wrap a new shampoo and conditioner for me so at least I would have something to open on Christmas morning. I remember holding back tears while unwrapping the shampoo. I was proud of my parents for doing what they felt they were supposed to be doing. However, the realization hit me; my parents were no longer my source. Although it was such an odd time in my life, God taught me such a valuable lesson. He taught me that He is my source for all things, needs, and wants alike. My parents had fulfilled their role in raising me. They had met my needs, just like responsible parents should. However, now it was time for me to learn these things on my own.

I remember not having a single penny to my name. Attending Texas Bible Institute, my faith was being stretched financially. Did I really believe God would supply all of my needs? I was running out of toothpaste, and obviously, this was not okay. Bible school students are annoying as it is. They cannot afford to also have stinky breath. Not to mention, I was also single. Therefore, brushing my teeth was even more vital to my marital goals. Sitting on my bed in the dormitory, I was embarrassed to ask my roommate for a pair of scissors to cut open my current toothpaste tube to scrape the last bit out. Frustrated, I told the Lord, "I know You are my Source, but in all honesty, from this viewpoint, it looks like my Source is slacking a bit. I need toothpaste, and You said in Your Word that You would supply all of my needs. Lord, this is a need, so I trust You to supply it."

At that moment, I sensed the Lord reminding me that what I sowed was what I would reap. It was in that moment that I awakened to the lie I had believed. I was poor. Therefore, I believed I had nothing to give. A victim mentality had rooted itself within my belief system. I had been walking around as needy instead of as a need meeter. Although, it is true that I had no money to give, I did have other seeds within my hands. I had time and a healthy body that could serve others. This meant I had plenty of seed to sow! So, that is just what I did. Over that next season, I began to sow whatever I could. I would do my roommates' chores. I would help fold people's clothes. I would carry other students' lunch trays to the trash area. Night after night, I would sweep the shared hallway in the dorm. Whatever I could find to sow, I did it. I was constantly looking around to find some sort of seed to plant in my garden.

It didn't feel spiritual or anointed or even easy. It was work, inconvenient, and sometimes, even embarrassing. However, thought by thought, I took captive anything that didn't line up with God bringing a financial harvest in my life. Then, action by action, I kept planting seed. The Bible tells us that He supplies seed to the sowers, and dang it, that is just what He did. I started recognizing more and more opportunities to serve people. Then actual paying odd jobs began to pop up. Next, opportunities to minister started to arise. Before I knew it, God had supplied me with a ministry job that paid the actual, real life kind of dollars. I was finally able to plant money seeds in my garden. So, sow I did. I can guarantee you that some of my husband's and my monetary success today is directly related to the spiritual shift that took place in my heart over a lack of toothpaste on that day. To this day, we are always sowing something. Big, small, tiny, or huge, seed is constantly being planting in the ground. This type of giving becomes reflexive. It is just who we are. We are givers, so we give. It has become our nature.

The next type of giving we do is purposeful giving. This is the giving we intentionally pray about, sense God speak about, or seek out. For us, it started with small things. We would hear of a family going through a hard time and sense the Lord nudging us to buy them groceries. So, we would.

Different from the reflexive giving, this is something that we actually feel in our hearts to do. We have had many things in our hearts to give. Can I just tell you right here how fun this kind of giving is? It is way more fun than buying anything for yourself! I mean, the Bible called it first; I am not the original author of this theory. Remembering the words the Lord Jesus himself said in Acts 10:35, "It is more blessed to give than to receive," it almost makes me just giddy thinking on how much excitement, joy, and life is deposited whenever we have the honor of blessing someone.

I remember the first car we were able to buy for a sweet family. I remember exactly where we were standing when we told them of our intentions. I am pretty sure we all cried and most definitely sure that we cried way more than they did. They weren't sad tears because our money was gone. They were tears that were rooted in the awe of God. How was it that He could take this girl who had to pray for a tube of toothpaste and this guy who had mostly bleached hand me downs as a kid and make them the conduit of His provision? It was by His grace and by His kingdom's system. We have learned and are still learning to yield to His kingdom's ways. We have given multiple cars since that day, and it honestly hasn't lost its luster yet. Now I feel like I "get" Oprah a little bit better.

The more we allow ourselves to be His vessels, the better we get at listening accurately to the Holy Spirit in this realm. Have we missed it at times? Yes. We have jumped the gun and we have given prematurely. We have also given out of compulsion or for man's praise. There have been times we even ignored God's gentle nudge to give and justified it by our own selfish excuses. It has been a journey to navigate through learning to hear accurately. As we weed out our selfish ambitions. God usually speaks to us through a gentle nudge, a slight prompting, or a tender whisper. However, there have also been times God has woken us up in the middle of the night to reveal needs in other continents that He wanted us to take care of.

The fact is, if we aren't careful, we can over complicate things. He is a good God who wants to use His people to meet others' needs. So surely if someone is crying out, "Lord, use me," He is happy to do so. As you and I make ourselves available for Him to use anything we have to do whatever He deems necessary, He will begin to use us. So ask Him to reveal needs to you that He wants you to meet. He will! His system is set up to meet the needs of His people through you, while blessing you.

God hears the prayers of His people, and He coordinates His children to be His hands and feet to answer these prayers. I am thinking of one missionary family specifically who have given their lives to spread the gospel to the people of Asia. The Braze's are a family of four who helps lepers, orphans and sex trafficking victims. Andrew Braze ventures into the most remote mountainous villages. The conditions these lepers are living in are gut wrenching, even sickening to see. The Braze's have rescued enslaved sex-trafficked victims, kept babies from being aborted, and built water facilities in leper colonies. The work they are doing is selfless and eternally fruitful.

Honestly, I had no idea the Braze's even existed until a few years ago. Steven was Facebook acquaintances with Andrew, but this was the extent of their relationship. Late one evening, the Lord put it on my husband's heart to ask Andrew Braze what he needed. Steven told Andrew that whatever need he had, we were to meet that need. At that time, Andrew's need was a lot heftier than other needs we were accustomed to meeting. However, Steven had heard from God, so I was on board. Andrew told Steven the need, and we were able to meet it quickly. Do you know after we met that need, the Braze's were able to literally multiply their reach? One very soon, very real day in heaven, we will have the honor of meeting former lepers who have said yes to Jesus, because we said yes to giving that day. In light of eternity, the monetary sacrifice seems so small compared to the eternal outcome. There will be people in heaven because we said "yes".

The yeses didn't start with the big things. The yeses started before we had any money to give. You can say yes now too! Not a penny to give, say yes to serving! Say yes to writing an encouraging note. Volunteer your time and skills. Being a good steward over a little promotes you to the opportunity of being a steward over much. Do your best to take care of what you have in your hands right now. By doing this, you are creating an avenue for God to multiply what you are stewarding.

His master replied, "Well done, good and faithful servant! You have been faithful with a few things; I will put you in charge of many things. Come and share your master's happiness!"
Matthew 25:23 (NIV)

Stop, and ask yourself the following questions:

Do you consider yourself more of a need needer or need meeter at this point in your life? Why?

What is one seed you have in your hand that you can sow today?

Write down one time you saw God's faithfulness to grow a seed you had planted.

Father, I ask you to help me see the seeds that I have in my life right now. Show me when and where to give specifically, as well as open my eyes to opportunities to give reflexively. Help me to see myself as a need-meeter and not as needy. Thank you. Amen.

RELEASE ALL ASSUMPTIONS AND JUDGMENTS TOWARD OTHERS' FINANCES

*"To those who judge others,
I offer this prophetic advice 'Stop it!'"*
— DIETER F. UCHTDORF

Excess, by definition, is to go beyond the usual, necessary, or proper limit or degree. So I ask you, by whose standards shall we compare to determine if what we have is proper or excess? Shall we choose the most destitute beggar to compare ourselves to? Then we are all in trouble, including Jesus who had His own treasurer. Excess is a relative term, which I am unsure whether anyone except the Lord Himself is fit to define.

It is far too easy to decide what is excessive when it comes to the way other people spend their money. How many of those purses does she have? Those clothes are way too expensive. Don't they know how many people they could feed with that ring on her finger? Why do they need a plane; do they think they are too good for commercial flights? Their house is way too big. Why do they need that many cars? Their living sure seems excessive. This list, these thoughts, and these judgments can go on and on. Judging other people's money will leave you spiraling down the wrong path quicker than you can say "Louis Vuitton." But on the flip side of the coin, it is all too easy to justify our own negative spending habits.

If you are still feeling like you need to be the Christianity money police of the world, let me help you with one little statement: You don't know it all! This statement has set me free.

First, You don't know what they have purchased and what has been given to them. You also don't know how much they have given to others. You don't know what kind of deal they may have received. You don't know their heart behind the purchase, nor do you know the sacrifices they have made to attain the things they have. You just don't know it all, and you never will. Since you don't know it all, you are no authority on their giving. Let this release you from even having an opinion on what other people have, and please surrender your money police badge immediately.

I was reading a very liked and gifted Christian author. This author was seriously on point, and she was so funny. It was as if she was my soul mate or my spirit animal. I was so thrilled to read her new book. Reading her book was like opening a present on Christmas morning as a kid or having latte with a best friend while wearing a cozy scarf; it was just simply fuzzy and magical. I found myself not wanting there to be an end to anything she wrote. Her wit, transparency, and sense of humor was a refreshing change from some of the beige, holy, snoozeable Christian authors that can sometimes flood the market. However, the magic quickly began to fade as I continued to read her new book. As I approached the third chapter, I was dumbfounded by the harsh criticism she was voicing towards fellow believers and their money. It was as if she had vomited all over the pages I was ingesting. I could tell we would be breaking up quickly.

The author was criticizing a handful of famous ministers. The specific critique was about their spending and the prosperity message. The author personally felt their prosperity was excessive and unnecessary and that the "materialism" misrepresented Christ. She called these ministers by name, one of whom happens to be related to one of my dear friends. The difference between this author and me was that I knew the true generosity of the person she had bashed. She harshly critiqued their spending from a distance, while I knew of their excessive generosity up close. What that author had voiced was completely untrue and downright hurtful. That author didn't know it all. Although she felt the cause burning within her to set the church world straight, it was an unjust, prideful cause that was completely unfounded. Had she known what I knew, she would never have written such filthy words towards such generous people. Plus, I am sure to many, her own spending seems excessive. Honestly, we reek of judgment when we decide what the acceptable standard of wealth is. Again, excessive spending is always relative.

Let's not religiously snub how others spend their big money, while we struggle with how to spend our little money. Who are we to think that we should decide how others use their money, whenever stewarding our own money can be a struggle?

While materialism and excess are real and can even become sinful problems within the body of Christ, unless you are in a close relationship with someone (as well as feel led by the Lord), I challenge you to let the Holy Spirit speak to someone's heart if they need to be corrected. Money is a very, very personal thing.

I have been on both sides of negative assumptions concerning finances. I have unjustly spoken against people's monetary habits. I have also been unjustly spoken about. Frankly, it is quite stripping on the latter side. In a sense, being judged regarding your personal finances is suffocating. On one hand, you want to justify yourself by explaining your heart, the sacrifices you've made, as well as how you have helped others. On the other hand, to talk about finances in such a way comes across as distasteful and braggadocios. Sometimes, your only choice is to say nothing and let God wash your name clean of the mud it has been dragged through.

There were moments in my younger life where I thought I really had it figured out concerning money. I knew how others, mainly everyone, specificially all the people could and should have spent their money. Somehow, I felt that I had the right to diagnose other people's excess. God bless Jamie Beth Jones, circa 2003. The fact is, especially in America, we all have more than so many others in the world. We all live excessively according to someone else's opinion. I hate to tell you this, dear reader, but it really comes down to a pride issue. Who am I to judge what someone else does with what they have? Let God spank His own, my friend. If the Lord needs to bring correction to one of His children, don't you know He is capable? If you have a sincere concern about someone and their finances, then you should sincerely pray for them. If I am not willing to take time to pray for someone, I tend to question how sincere my concern on the matter really is.

Not only is it not our call to define what excess means for others, but it is just plain dumb to try to do so. If you are reading this book, you want to be rich. And, if you aren't already, hopefully by the time you finish reading this book, you will want to be rich for the right reasons. Assuming you have the correct motives, if I were you, I would begin sowing grace to the all of the folks who are rich right now. Do this for two reasons, number one, mercy triumphs over judgment (His words, not mine). Mercy is always better. Mercy is not always the fairest or easiest way, but rest assured, it beats being judgmental every time. Number two, you will reap what you sow. Each word sown towards others is a seed planted in two gardens, yours and theirs. What you say will affect them as well as you. Dear friend, strongly consider if your harsh criticisms of others are needed and necessary before you plant them. One day, the one who is harvesting those harsh seeds just may be you.

Division is a sneaky tool of the enemy to handicap the body of Christ. He knows that the world will know us by our love. Therefore, he takes great effort to shadow our love with unforgiveness and acidic judgments towards each other. So speak kindly towards those who are rich today, the words you want to be spoken over your little rich self tomorrow. Selah.

Do not judge, or you too will be judged. For in the same way you judge others, you will be judged, and with the measure you use, it will be measured to you. Why do you look at the speck of sawdust in your brother's eye and pay no attention to the plank in your own eye? How can you say to your brother,

"Let me take the speck out of your eye," when all the time there is a plank in your own eye? You hypocrite, first take the plank out of your own eye, and then you will see clearly to remove the speck from your brother's eye.

Matthew 7:1-5 (NIV)

Take a moment to reflect on the following questions:

Can you think of a person whose financial decision you have judged?

What can you pray about for that person today?

Think of something kind you can do for someone who has more than you.

Father, forgive me for judging the way others have spent their money. I ask that you would remind me to pray for people, when I feel the draw to condemn them. Lord, help me to plant good words and lots of mercy concerning those who are well off. Amen.

MAKE RADICAL MOVES WHEN IT SEEMS RIGHT

"You have to crack an egg to make an omelet."
—GLENN FULKERSON

Taking risks is a foundational principle for most self-made, wealthy people. As a believer, you have inside information from the Head of all intelligence. There may be times when you feel like you are supposed to make an out of the box decision. It may not line up with the most conservative of choices. Do it anyway. Taking risks and living bravely will open more doors of opportunity to accumulating wealth than living super cautiously ever will. As you learn to listen to the leading of the Holy Spirit, as well as allow mentors to speak into your life, taking risks will eventually evolve into excitement over fear.

There is always an element of the unknown that can toy with your emotions. However, when you let God lead your decisions, you will be settled into peace. You won't need to know the exact final outcome, nor will you have to have every step laid out perfectly. If He is leading you to make a radical move, put on your big kid

Underoos and just do it. You may be scared, your voice may shake, but bravely walk out the plans and steps He has for you.

Sometimes, we have missed it. There were times we thought we had peace about something, and then we fell flat on our faces. We had to pick ourselves up, dust our bruised financial rears off, and keep on keeping on. God, being rich in mercy, has always led us to victory—even when it took us a while to get there. He caused us to triumph in our finances. See, God knew that even in our human, erred ways, our hearts always wanted to please Him in the choices we were making. So, He gave grace. He gave grace to start over, grace to be restored, and grace to succeed again. Even the times we wanted something He didn't want and we went our own way, as soon as we yielded our hearts and ways to Him, His super lovingkindness and mercy rescued us again. Man, I love Him and His underserved grace.

Steven has taught me so much about risk. To be quite honest, I would have been super comfortable with Steven being a mid-level manager with a stable 401k for the rest of our lives. Him, not so much. He was thriving in his position at a successful construction company in San Antonio. He had godly mentors, and he enjoyed being with his colleagues. We had just had our first child, and life was steady-eddie and beautifully predictable. He left after breakfast, and He was home for dinner. We knew exactly what our paycheck would be, and the day we would be paid. We could budget and plan out all of our finances for the whole year. It was nice, clean, and tidy. Then that whole "made for more" thing began to rise up in Steven. It was at this point that the hunger for purpose began to grow in him. Parallel timing to this new hunger within Steven, he was asked to take a sales position at the company. It would be a commission-only position. This meant if he didn't sell, we didn't eat. It didn't seem like a wise choice at the time. We had just had our first baby, and the consistent paycheck carried such a nice sense of stability. But the prompting on Steven's heart to do sales was more than he could ignore. Eventually I also had peace about it, even in the midst of uncertainty. So, we went for it.

The first few months were like watching a baby giraffe walk for the first time. It took a moment for us to feel steady or comfortable. However, looking back, I can see how taking that one risky step laid the foundation for the success we have seen God bring about in our lives. Steven grew quickly as a salesperson and became quite good at it. We began to give bigger than we ever had before. In return, we were harvesting more than we ever had before. We were able to pay off our house within two years of purchase. Had we chosen to remain cozy within our predictable life, that would never have happened. At this point, we were in our twenties and on top of the world, living debt free!

Right in the crescendo of Steven's sales success, I could smell change in the air. We had just had our second child when God put a desire in Steven to move back to his hometown, Tulsa, and start his own business. Hold the phone, and cue the dialogue within my head. *Our own business? As in, nobody will be paying for our insurance? As in, use our savings to start it? As in, we could lose literally all of our financial stability? As in, we have never done this before? As in, leave Texas? As in, no more breakfast tacos?*

This time, this was a harder pill for me to swallow. The only experience we had with starting our own business was the two times before, early on in our marriage, when we had failed. That's right F-A-I-L-E-D. As in humiliating, we weren't good enough, we missed it, we lost money, failed.

However, I knew that I couldn't let fear lead me. I had a knowing on the inside that this was our next step. When my mind would begin to race, I would sit in God's presence and the peace that He provided would quiet my racing heart. Besides, as much as I respected my husband and his position as a leader within our family, he was not my source. God was. He always had been, He always would be. I was in covenant with Him. I knew no matter what, God would take care of us. We were faithful tithers and givers. We had plenty seed in the ground. I knew that even if we lost it all, His nature is grace and provision, so we would be okay.

As a believer, taking risks is about faith and trust. Each risky choice is our own walk on the water moment. If we hear God calling, even if it doesn't seem to make sense or there seems to be no way it will ever work, we must trust. Trust that He is for us, not against us. Trust that He is smarter than us and knows the end from the beginning. And if we happen to miss it and begin to sink, trust that He will rescue us.

There is a whole lot more fulfillment in saying "Yes" to whatever He may ask us to do, wherever He may ask us to go, and whenever He may ask us to do it. If your dream is to land on the moon, you have to be willing to get in the spaceship. The answer is not to pray that your gravity laden sedan will get you there. We can sit in our car and hope, pray, confess, and believe it will go to the moon. That car isn't going to the moon. Maintaining and growing wealth

God's way requires that we take risks, seek Him, and obey when we hear Him. Praying that God will increase your finances without being willing to do whatever He says is a prayer prayed in vain. He knows the vehicle that will take you on the road you need to be on, to get you to where you need to be, to meet the people you need to meet, to do the stuff that needs doing, in order to increase you. However, if you are not willing to get out of your comfortable, padded, safe way of doing things, I can almost guarantee you, you will find yourself facing an early economic plateau.

> **Trust in and rely confidently on the Lord with all your heart and do not rely on your own insight or understanding. In all your ways know and acknowledge and recognize Him, and He will make your paths straight and smooth.**
>
> **Proverbs 3:5-6 (AMP)**

Taking risks that you deem worthy to take is not a sure way to gain wealth; taking risks you feel peace about and/or His leading on is. In everything you do, acknowledge God. If He handles your eternal well being with grace and precision, surely He can handle your business ventures. The Bible is full of scriptures about prayer. There are loads of verses that tell us that whenever we talk, He listens. Over and over, there are stories of people crying out to our God who faithfully has a listening ear. Taking a risk as a shot in the dark will get you nowhere fast. The good news is, as believers, we don't have to! In James, we are instructed to boldly ask for wisdom. Whenever we ask Him, He gives it to us. In fact, the Bible says he freely and liberally gives us wisdom. He gives us a big portion and plenty of it. He isn't stingy with His ways and thinking. He is ready to give you His insight.

As I type these words, I pray you don't receive them casually. I pray you soberly grasp that our God is listening, the One who created all of the heavens, planets, solar systems, oceans, creatures, earth, man, and woman merely by His words. This is the God who is longing to have you ask Him for wisdom so He can liberally download it into you.

Sit and think on this. How powerful is He that He can split a sea? How miraculous is He that He can raise the dead? How genius is He that He can put the solar systems in motion? How personal is He that He knows the number of hairs on our heads? How loving is He that He sent His Son to die for you, so that there would be nothing separating you and Him? This is the God you are praying to. He has silenced wars, healed cancer, mended broken hearts and restored impossible marriages. He is full of the potent power able to change the whole world in an instant. He is an endless resource at our disposal. So, please, get the reality of this. Our very real God is very willing to lead you. All you have to do is ask, listen, and obey. We can leave the hard stuff to Him.

Are you willing to leave the hard stuff to him? Take a moment to answer the following questions for yourself:

What are some ways you have seen the Lord work things out in your life?

Have you been feeling His prompting to step out in faith and take a "risk" in your finances?

What is the first step to take in following that prompting?

Lord, help us overcome our fear of the unknown. Let our decisions be guided by You as You lead us into peace. We recognize that you have never failed us and will never do so. And we thank You for Your underserved grace and love that picks us up when we fall and helps us keep going. Thank You that You are our source, and we choose today to put our trust in you and follow your leading. Amen.

CREATE A CULTURE OF LEARNING

"Build your skill, show up, and be steady. It is amazing what God can do with a person that will just keep showing up."

– CHARLIE DANIELS

Through wisdom is a house built; and by understanding it is established: and by knowledge shall the chambers be filled with all precious and pleasant riches.

Proverbs 24:3 (KJV)

I am all for hard work, faithfulness, and consistency. However, left alone, it is an incomplete formula. Without adding a process and culture for attaining knowledge, you will stifle your capacity for wealth. By stifling your capacity for wealth, you hinder your true gospel reach.

Learning should be a lifelong process. I hate to break this to you, but on this side of eternity, you will never know it all. As long as you are here on this earth, there is never a finish line as far as learning is concerned. One key to attaining wealth is to keep your mental muscles moving. Absorbing what others know, in any subject, will increase your capacity. Whether you are studying your field of expertise or learning a hobby, the principle is the same. This is brain exercise. Learning expands your ability to accumulate wealth. Stretching your learning threshold in any particular subject enables you to grow in your own field as well. The more you know, the more valuable you are to others. Adding value to your expertise equates adding zeros to your paychecks.

Make it the norm to learn something daily. Create a culture of accumulating knowledge. These modern times that we live in are full of avenues to learn any subject. My husband is the expert at this. If he wants to know something, he will search until he finds it. He has read books, YouTube'd, googled, and sought out experts on many subjects. We are talking about a business man who specializes in construction here. However, ask him about photography, German engineered cameras, duck hunting, British history, marketing, guns, internet saturation, and now his latest, flying a plane, and he can talk shop.

Steven has grown into a true student of many things. He is a gatherer of facts. This in itself is a miracle. He is not a college graduate. Not to mention, his charm alone got him through even high school. Over the years, he has learned to value education. He pursues knowledge, and he has taught me to do the same. Our evenings aren't fogged with television shows and playing Bejeweled. A typical evening in our household consists of "How to" YouTube videos, reading, conversing, and listening to podcasts or sermons. This is our regular routine. It isn't that we don't watch a movie here and there, it's just that we have purposefully created this culture within our family. We don't learn in order to get richer; we learn in order to be better. Getting richer is a natural byproduct of being better. Steven and I both have our favorite ways to learn. Neither trumps the other. I am more of a reader and a podcast listener. He is more of a gatherer of resources like YouTube, online articles, and relational resources. People are often surprised to hear that we do not have cable. No, I have never seen *Parenthood*. No, I did not watch the game. No, my kid's don't know the latest show from the Disney Channel. The truth of the matter is, it has nothing at all to do with an ethical opposition to cable. The day simply doesn't allow time for us to watch television on a regular schedule. It is a culture we have diligently strived to build within our home.

The point is this, if learning is more of an isolated event and not so much your culture, you will stifle the potential you have to grow. If you can find a way to learn that you enjoy, learning feels more like sitting down for a good meal than doing the dishes. And we are all more likely to prioritize eating a good meal than doing those blast dishes. This may come by trial and error, and your preferred way of learning may change throughout the seasons of life. Just keep at it. Keep pursuing growth. Acquiring wealth is less about the knowledge attained and more about the journey in pursuing it. Realizing you are in a state of process enables God to grace you at whatever you are doing.

> **Most gladly, therefore, I will rather boast about my weaknesses, so that the power of Christ may dwell in me.**
> **2 Corinthians 12:9 (NASB)**

When we say, "God, I don't know all I need to know, but You do," we enable His power to work within us. Can we be done with inviting Him into our process and, instead, yield to His? This is one of the things that separates the extraordinary from the ordinary. Give everything you do, even the way you learn, to Him. Let Him grace you to grow.

Knowing you don't know it all is part of being humble. Realizing God can use other people and resources to teach you, opens the door for Him to exalt you. It is His system. James 4:10 (NASB) says, "Humble yourselves in the presence of the Lord, and He will exalt you."

Can we trust this process? Can we trust that it is okay for us to be in a place where we don't have all of the answers, know all of the ins and outs, or sometimes even right from wrong? It is in this place where we acknowledge the superiority of our God. As we lower our posture to one of learning, it is in this place He is able to exalt us. I have exalted myself, and I have had God exalt me. Rest assured, it is always better for Him to do the exalting. It is not about becoming an expert in every field. It is about using your mental capacity to the best of your ability, and calling on Him to help you do. To be quite honest, my Steven is a much faster learner than I am. He is not intimidated in the slightest bit to learn something new. He is a jump off the high-dive, do a flip on the way down, and crash right into that water kind of guy. He will engulf himself within a subject until he is fully saturated with it. He will talk about it, study it, and think about it over and over until he gets it. So help me if he tells me one more historical face about Billy the Kid, I am just over it. I, on the other hand, am more of a look at the water, dip my toe in, slowly ease down each step until my temperature regulates kind of gal. I have a tendency to be more intimidated at learning a new subject than he does. However, once I am in it, even if it takes me three years, I am all in it. I will research which book to buy about the subject, buy the book, read the book, highlight the book, read the highlights, then I will maybe, just maybe, bring it up in conversation. We have two totally different techniques.

God made us all different, and He did this for a reason. So whatever is more of your learning style, embrace and cater to it. There is no need to hinder your process because someone picks things up faster or easier than you. Some learning styles and speeds are not better than others, just different. Do something, lest you do nothing, my friend. Brick by brick, evening by evening, choice by choice, build that culture of learning. Let's be good stewards of the mental capacity God has given us. A learning culture is a growing culture.

Learning is essential, so stop and think about the following questions:

Have you stopped creating a culture of learning in your life?

Whether it be reading a book, watching a tutorial, or something else, what avenue of learning do you enjoy?

What resources are available to you within this avenue?

Father, help us to never stop learning and to create an environment and culture of learning within our homes and our lives. Help us to open our hearts and minds, not only to understanding but also to wisdom. Reveal to us new avenues of learning or people that we can draw knowledge from. We thank You that You go with us on this journey, and we yield our hearts and minds to Your process of learning and growing. In Jesus' name. Amen

UNDERSTAND THAT SACRIFICE IS PART OF THE PACKAGE DEAL

"Faith can move mountains...but don't be surprised if God hands you a shovel!"
— TERRI SAVELLE FOY

The soul of the sluggard craves, and gets nothing, while the soul of the diligent is richly supplied.

Proverbs 13:4 (RSV)

Anyone who has ever accumulated their own wealth has had to sacrifice in one way or another. It is part of the package deal. If you want a lifestyle of financial success, you are choosing a lifestyle of sacrifice. There are sacrifices we have made on both small and large scales that many people will never see. In fact, sometimes people's perceptions can be quite opposite of reality. Having wealth is often looked at as getting lucky. You fell into the cash! You found the golden ticket, plucked the four-leaf clover, and pulled the big piece of the wishbone, you lucky dog, you. Sometimes wealth is attributed exclusively to a person's gifting. Other times, it is solely attributed to God's favor. The truth of the matter is there is simply no luck about it. Although gifting has its place and we are grateful for everything God has placed inside of us, it is not the sole reason success comes.

There are plenty of poor, gifted people. God's favor may make up a large sum of the reason one becomes wealthy, but that is not the single way one can sustain wealth. For we are stewards, not hoarders, of His gifts and His blessings. If we are stewards, it means we have a hand in the outcome. If this were not so, would not all believers be financially wealthy? God is just and shows no partiality. So if wealth comes just because of God's favor alone, why would people from the same culture, same background, same opportunities, knowing the same God end up in different financial places? Submitting to God's system for increasing your finances is exactly that, submission. It is a yielding of one's way. Financial success God's way is a combination of His grace, your hard work, and plenty of sacrifice on the whole family's part.

I really do have to bite my tongue when people casually give luck credit for what God has done. Not only has God graced us to do what He has called us to do, but He has put systems in place from the foundation of the world that help to feed and maintain His will. As His steward, you have to realize that His system, which He created, is the only environment in which His giftings, talents, and favor will thrive. So even if I have done my part, it is in His system alone that success is cultivated.

It has been a joint effort for team Jones. We sacrifice the normal eight to five workday in order to be the best at what we do in our industry. There is no vacation in which we are ever truly unplugged from work. Three out of five (or more) weeknight dinners, Daddy is at an appointment. This means Momma solely does the cooking, dishes, bath times, helping with the homework, and putting of the kids to bed.

Along with being the boss, comes added pressures. You not only feel responsible for making a living for your family, but also for the families of your employees and subcontractors. Taxes, insurance, and legalities all become way more complicated. We work longer hours and adapt our schedule to fit the needs of clients, all the while trying to keep our family a priority. If no money is flowing into our business, we are the last to get paid, and there have been times we have gone in the red in order to pay our people, while we put nothing into our personal accounts. People often want what successful people have, but they aren't willing to do what successful people have done.

If you want to be wealthy God's way, you will never again buy what you can afford. Now, you must learn to live below your means. Leaving plenty of margin is key to financial freedom. This means buying less of a car and house than you can afford. Don't buy the house you can pay off in thirty years; buy the one you can pay off in ten. It is expensive to be rich and even more expensive to have a lot of assets. So choose your margin, and choose it wisely. When Steven and I got serious about getting rich, we didn't get more; we gave up more. I stopped getting my nails done. Steven sold his truck, and I even drove his mom and dad's old minivan with the added accessory of a leaking sunroof. Our budget was fierce. Three nights out of seven, we ate beans. Through the different seasons, the face of sacrifice has changed. Sometimes it was packing lunch for work, other times it was evenings spent couponing. Although always worth the added effort and sacrifice, it is not the easiest road to take. However, admittedly, delayed gratification is the most savory gratification there is.

Please understand, this is not your cordial invite to attend my rich girl's pity party. "Poor me, my latte gets cold sometimes whilst I get a hand massage." I just want to paint a clear picture of the reality of having more to steward. There is more sacrifice to growing in wealth than there is to remaining stagnant in your financial endeavors. This is why not everyone does it. You can't give up when things get difficult. When you have reached your pain threshold for growth, you must stretch some more. This is a marathon, you'll be in this race for a while. Going slow is an option, but giving up isn't.

Imagine that we take a random survey asking only this: Do you want to have more than enough money to live well and give well? I guarantee you, the overwhelming response would be an emphatic "Yes!" Now imagine asking those same people if they are willing to eat beans, drive leaky cars, and give up some family dinners to do so. Their answers might change a bit. The sacrifices you need to make are not too hard, yet they are still hard. Saying no to a few things today, means saying yes to better things tomorrow.

I basically raised my children alone until they were ages three and four, while my husband worked his tail off to get our first successful business off the ground. We have been sued, needed marriage counseling, and even lost some friends along the way. Admittedly, the biggest thing we have sacrificed is our comfort zone. Ugh, it seems just when we feel like we are beginning to actually get it, God stretches us a little bit more. It hasn't always been easy. However, it has all been worth it.

One thing that God has been working on in me is having a willing heart to make these sacrifices. Simply obeying and sacrificing isn't really enough. Jesus has always been after our hearts.

If you are willing and obedient, you shall eat the good of the land.

Isaiah 1:19 (KJV)

As a parent, the goal is not to get my children to do what I say because it shows me respect. As a parent, my goal is for my children to willingly do what I say because they trust that somehow it is for their benefit and I may just know what I am talking about sometimes. Is it not the same with God? To be willing is to acknowledge that He knows what is best. If I could go back in time, I would be a more willing wife when it came to running the household by myself. I would have had a sweeter heart when I was gallivanting around town in the minivan with a leaky ceiling. Having a willingness to sacrifice shows a tender and pure heart towards God. It reveals that we understand and trust the heart of our Father towards us. A willing heart shows that we know He has graced us with the ability to do each thing He has asked us to do. A willing heart acknowledges that it is not all about us, but it is all about Him and His purposes. A willing heart says, "I am happy to be on the team and be a part. I don't care if I am in the dugout, pitcher, or ball boy. I am grateful to wear the jersey."

God wants us to eat the good of the land. Who will be more

profitable for the kingdom of God, the one who has the worst vehicle that frequently breaks down or the one who has a good car in perfect running condition? How about the one who has enough to help the poor or the one who can't feed his own family? Well, the one with the good car and the extra money, of course! God has good intentions for us.

A willing heart is the purifier of all greed. If I am willing to hear God and do what He says, it proves that I know who the source of my finances is. I also know who my money really belongs to. They belong to Him and His purposes. A willing heart just wants to do what the Lord wants it to do. Maybe right now you don't have a willing heart in some areas. Honestly, I have been there many times. Let me ask you this, are you willing to have a willing heart? If you are, ask God for help. I know He will lead you into being willing. If we are honest with ourselves, I would say we have all had moments in which we are unwilling to be uncomfortable. After a while, sacrifice can lose its romanticism and become all too real. This is where you are not only okay but encouraged to be stubborn. This is where you keep on keeping on. God is so clear in His Word. You will have your harvest; you just can't give up. Remain consistent and steady with your eyes on the prize. Sacrifice may be part of the package, but it is worth each drop of sweat, every tear cried, and all of the moments you have invested. His timing is perfect! At the proper time, you will reap your harvest.

Let us not become weary in doing good, for at the proper time we will reap a harvest if we do not give up.

Galatians 6:9 (NIV)

Take a moment to grow your stewardship with the following questions:

Are you being a steward or a hoarder with your money?

In what areas of your life are you living beyond your means?

What can you say "no" to today, so that you can say "yes" later?

6

Father, I ask that You would reveal to us any areas in our hearts that are not willing right now. Help us to rejoice in the opportunity to sacrifice, because we know that You know exactly what You are doing. I ask that each seed sown would be sown with a pure heart, reflecting only trust and admiration towards You. Give us strength to keep going, with our eyes on You. We thank You that at the right, proper time, our harvest will be ready. In Jesus' name, Amen.

MAKE YOUR "WHY" BIGGER THAN YOUR PAIN

(VIEW MONEY AS A RESOURCE, NOT A GOAL)

"The motive is not to be rich, but to gain a position of greater influence."

— ALEX ISER

The whole point to God's system of getting wealth is that once you attain it, you will do what He wants you to do with it. Sometimes, really getting this can make for a long and hard journey. Sometimes, the sacrifices that need to be made are so loud, they seem to drown out the purpose behind them. This is why your "why" must be big. In fact, I would say your "why" must be really big. Why do you want the money? What is your purpose for pursuing wealth? Which problems were you created to solve? What injustice makes your blood boil? What causes are you willing to fight for? What sets you afire? Is there a thing that ignites your very core?

At the end of the day, what we are all called to do is to know God and point people to Him. Whether we are teachers, entrepreneurs, police officers, stay at home moms, secretaries, builders, pastors, or body builders, our core purpose for existence is all the same: to know Him and to make Him known. The "why" behind everything we do must echo this call to humanity. Our "why," whether general or specific, must be crashing and abrasive to a dormant life. The cry to make a difference must swell up inside of us enough to cause us to push through when things get hard. To truly make Jesus Lord of your life is to surrender and bow all motives and aspirations before Him. We don't acquire wealth so that we can have more, do more, impress more. The pursuit of wealth is not about attaining the Escalade or the Rolex. If it was a watch we were aiming for, we would have quit a long time ago. We personally acquire wealth so that we can reach more souls with the saving gospel message of Jesus.

This side of eternity really is so extremely short. It is just a mist, here for a quick moment, then gone. The sobering reality that drives us is that each person in times past, present, and future will live forever. Whether they will live forever in a very real heaven or a just as real hell hangs on one factor: their acceptance of our Lord, Jesus Christ. Eternity is long. To think that God would empower me to gain wealth so I could help send someone to share the eternity-altering message of the gospel is quite humbling.

The Father longs to be with each of us forever. The initial intended fellowship in the garden was just a glimpse of the intimacy that awaits us in eternity. One day, we will be able to see Him face to face and worship Him in unveiled truth. This is His heart for all of humanity. Every tribe, people group, age, gender, and nation is longed for by the Father. I pray people would see their need for a Savior who waits to unite them with Himself within an atmosphere of perfect love and peace. The alternative is as dark as dark gets. No life or light, hell awaits with fire, pain, and separation from God. There is no second chance or earning your way up from there. Once we meet that side of eternity, our choice has been made.

Our "why" is to reach as many people as we can with God's love on this side, so they never have to see hell on that side. This is something that will get you out of bed in the morning. Herein lies our motivation to keep sowing and keep plowing. Our heart is that we will maximize our true gospel reach. We want to be the best stewards to reach as many people as we can, even when it hurts.

It all sounds so holy though, doesn't it? Hear me loud and clear here. This does not mean we walk around in sackcloth and ashes, parading about with some false humility that boasts of not having a retirement fund because we trust in God and have given everything away. No, in fact, I believe the Lord delights in blessing His children.

The blessing of the Lord makes rich, and he adds no sorrow with it.
Proverbs 10:22 (ESV)

This Book of the Law shall not depart from your mouth, but you shall meditate on it day and night, so that you may be

careful to do according to all that is written in it. For then you will make your way prosperous, and then you will have good success.

Joshua 1:8 (ESV)

If you then, being evil, know how to give good gifts to your children, how much more will your Father who is in heaven give what is good to those who ask Him!

Matthew 7:11 (NASB)

God has given us good gifts to enjoy. If the enemy can't keep you from wealth, he will surely try to keep you from enjoying it. We must refuse condemnation. There is no room in my walk with God for condemnation. Guilt has no right to take up occupancy in my thoughts. I can enjoy what God has freely given to me. While I want to encourage you, too, to enjoy what God so freely gives and even delights in giving us, I also think it's time we talk about the flip side.

What should not be your "why": Money itself. The love of money is a thing. Like, a very real thing. A very real, bad thing. A hideous thing that will suffocate the life right out of you. Nobody really talks about this in the prosperity camp, which I still feel a part of. It is not evidence of a lack of faith nor does it show unbelief to take heed in guarding your heart against the pure evil of the love of money. Hear me when I tell you that wanting money for money's sake is defeating in and of itself. It is easy to crave the stuff that money can buy. It is human nature to want what you can't have. However, it is not God's best. Loving money can get you off course quickly, doing much damage to every aspect of your life. The love of money is a selfish mindset that slowly molds you into a reservoir of assets, instead of a conduit of resources as God intends.

Don't store up treasures here on earth where they can erode away or may be stolen. Store them in heaven where they will never lose their value and are safe from thieves. If your profits are in heaven, your heart will be there too. If your eye is pure, there will be sunshine in your soul. But if your eye is clouded with evil thoughts and desires, you are in deep spiritual darkness. And oh, how deep that darkness can be! You cannot serve two masters: God and money. For you will hate one and love the other, or else the other way around.

Matthew 6:19 (TLB)

The problem is, nobody except you can know if money has you. It is impossible to know if someone has fallen prey to the love of money by what they have, because you never know what they are willing to give. So, this is one of those "come to Jesus" meetings we must have often. On purpose, we have to evaluate our own hearts. The more successful I become financially, the more I must have honest moments where I examine my true feelings in this area. Dear God, I don't ever want to ever put my material assets above someone else's eternal outcome.

I honestly wanted to leave these scriptures out of this chapter. I thought it might be too much messy and too much gray to dissect in such a forum. However, if we are going to believe the Word of God, we are going to believe the whole Word of God. We cannot pick and choose the parts of the Bible that fit our nice and neat, tidy theology and call it sound doctrine. Embracing all of what the Word says will bring freedom and clarity, even in the midst of not understanding it all. When Jesus came, He brought with Him such grace for the mistakes that we would make with our fleshly bodies. However, His challenge for our hearts is even louder than the one for our obvious outward sins. I believe a common thread of the New Testament is to examine our hearts in all things. What motivates me? What is my "why"? Which side of eternity am I affecting more?

These are all vital questions for which we must have answers. Only God knows if we are being honest about how surrendered we truly are. You could probably fool me, and I could probably fool you. But there is no fooling the One who fashioned our inner parts.

When the going gets tough in this journey to becoming financially successful, wanting a new house, designer purse, or luxury car will never be enough to keep gas in your motivational tank. Only a clear call to impact eternity can fuel your true purpose. I must admit, there is such a delicate balance to enjoying the Father's blessings without condemnation on this side of eternity, while focusing on reaching others for that side of eternity. There is no clear cut scale or formula to know if you are doing it right. Dang it, I wish there was an app for that! What I do know is God knows, and since He knows, He will help us know. If we can continue to be honest with ourselves and examine our hearts, He will lead us into the right balance for whatever season we are in. He leads and guides us into all truth, even truth concerning money.

We have all heard it said, "Having money isn't wrong, but money having you is." Honestly, Steven and I really don't have to beat ourselves up over making sure that stuff doesn't have us. Money is not our true goal. Money is a resource we can use to accomplish our real goal. We see ourselves as vessels that God can fill with talents and resources as He sees fit. As the resources flow through our vessels, God uses them to impact others while at the same time, blessing us. For instance, if I have a jar of honey and I pour some of that honey in a jar to give to you, will there not still be honey left in my jar? Of course there will be! This is the heart of our Father, He always has more than enough.

Steven and I are both quick to give away anything that we find ourselves taking our identity in or priding ourselves in. Trying hard to not love money is not what keeps us in line. We stay free from the love of money because we don't forget our "why." We want to see as many people as we can cross that eternal line, straight into heaven's pearly gates. Our heart is burdened to think of the lost remaining lost. There is no room for the love of money in our hearts, when the love of converted souls is constantly in our sight.

Seek first the kingdom of God and his righteousness, and all of these things (clothes, food, shelter, needs) will be added unto you.

Matthew 6:33 (ESV)

Take a moment to examine your "Why":

Why does God want you to have wealth?

Take a moment to examine your heart. What is your reason for getting money?

Are you both giving and enjoying your wealth at this time in your life?

Father, I ask that we would be tender to your leading. May our hearts beat with the cause of Christ. Open our eyes that we may see the desperation within humanity for a savior. Lord, as we continue to grow in wealth, help our motives remain pure and on track. Let the reason for wealth be to reach the unreached and help those in need. Amen.

BE CONTENT AND GRATEFUL

*"The moment you start acting like life is a blessing,
it starts feeling like one."*

— DR. DAVE MARTIN

Hebrews 13:5 (KJV) lays it out plainly: "Let your conversation be without covetousness; and be content with such things as ye have: for he hath said, I will never leave thee, nor forsake thee."

There is such a fine line between being content and being complacent. Contentment is being peaceful and happy in the current reality of your situation. Contentment refuses to be unsatisfied and rejects the feeling of lack. Content people are grateful and satisfied, knowing that God is in control no matter what. It is in knowing this we find a place to be totally satisfied. Being content does not means you lack ambition or fight. In fact, it means quite the opposite. Godly contentment embraces the journey, knowing that wherever we are is just fine, because God has our best interests in mind and He is working on our behalf. While we can't let circumstances steal our joy, we can still change our circumstances.

Contentment is a healthy view, while complacency leads to a dangerous fall.

A person who is complacent is satisfied with mediocrity. There is no inward drive to go bigger or do better. It just is. While contentment speaks of gratitude, complacency speaks of selfishness. It says, "I have enough for me, so that is enough." Contentment says, "I am grateful for my current view, I will stay forever if that is where He leads me. However, I wonder what is behind that mountain?"

> **For I have learned in whatever state I am, to be content: I know how to be abased, and I know how to abound. Everywhere and in all things I have learned both to be full and to be hungry, both to abound and to suffer need. I can do all things through Christ who strengthens me.**
>
> **Philippians 4:11-13 (NKJV)**

Paul leads us to a scriptural monetary view: In all things, I am content. Notice the source of strength. It is God! A content person is strengthened by Him. A complacent person fuels from within, which eventually leads to outward depletion. When you see yourself as your own source, you have no option but to be done because you have limits. However, when God is your source, you are limitless. Therefore, you can be content in your state, because it is ever changing as He leads you. Complacency says, "I am good here. All of my needs are met. I have got this." I hate feeling alone, like it is all up to me and all for me. It is such a defeating mindset. The difference between being content with little and being complacent with little is there are two different destinations.

Contentment is still moving forward as He leads. Complacency has already arrived at its destination.

Journeying toward your goals can cause much frustration. I do not want to discount the fact that it can be hard, and there have been times I have said, "I don't flipping even want to do this." One the hardest times of my life was when we were starting the business. My children were born eighteen months apart, so I had a nine month old and a just past two year old. I knew we had heard from God. I felt like a single mom. The kids only saw their daddy on the weekends, due to his schedule. This meant every naptime, bedtime, bath time, and mealtime was all up to me. Every cuddle, discipline, sick day, cranky day, and teething day, it was just me. There were no breaks once daddy got home because he was worn out, and let's be honest, moms just don't stop. I took out the trash, gassed up the car, did the grocery shopping, and cleaned the house. Emotionally I was drained, spent, and even almost bitter towards God or Steven or maybe both, I don't know. There were moments when I had to stop, breathe, and search to be content. I had to search for anything worthy of gratitude. It felt like my marriage was unraveling, along with my sanity.

At this point, we were using our savings to get the business going, so there were no guarantees of financial success. Looking back, I can see how I totally missed the mark of contentment and gratitude in that season. Don't get me wrong, I loved being a mom, but I hated parenting alone. I think had I called on God's grace, that season could have looked a lot different. I feel like my ungrateful attitude fixed my gaze on me, myself, and I. I became selfish and a complacent victim of my circumstances. Instead of focusing on being a cheerleader for my man and stability for my children, my focus was on me, poor Jamie, the girl nobody takes care of. The only reason I have no regrets is because of the valuable lessons I learned. I think this is when I truly learned to see every glass as half full. Survival mode kicked in, and I had to.

If I could go back and talk to that Jamie, I would tell her that there are billions of people in the world who would trade places with her in an instant. I would remind her that if all she has to thank God for is two healthy babies, then that should be enough to praise Him all day. I would tell her she is made for these moments, and she thrives when things get hard. I would tell her little preacher butt to do what she told countless others to do, "Seek God, and don't stop until you've found your peace." I would tell her that although she feels like nobody ever takes care of her, she should not be so quick to forget a God who promises comfort, strength, and sanity. I would remind her that no selfless act goes unnoticed by her heavenly Father. Then I would tell her to put on her big girl panties and get back in the game! I would tell her to let love be her aim. For when we aim to love, and not to be loved, somehow, God takes care of both.

It is funny how we think of gratitude as being something our circumstances influence. We think the people who have the assets, steady businesses, or good positions should be the most grateful. However, gratitude comes from within, despite the circumstances. Choosing to be grateful will shift your perception of the very place you are in. It doesn't matter what your circumstance looks like, thanking God can reframe anything you are going through. If you can choose to be thankful, you have just unlocked a door for God to bless you. Gratitude speaks of trust and humility, and don't you know Our God delights in those?

Sometimes, Steven and I wake up and say, "How did we get here?" We both know it is all God. Our gratitude for the experiences we've had the privilege of being a part of far exceeds our love for any stuff we may own. The relationships God has put in our path are some of the most valuable assets we have ever had. I could write another book filled with all of the good things God has done for us, and possibly another on all of the junk the world has brought, but alas, I am grateful for all of it.

And we know that in all things God works for the good of those who love him, who have been called according to his purpose.

Romans 8:28 (NIV)

Friends, I have learned to be grateful for even the junk now. I am better because of the crapola I have walked through. I am stronger, braver, and more willing to live fully now. God has somehow turned everything around. Through His amazing mercy and relentless love, He has reformatted the worst of things to benefit us. I don't know how He does it, but He just does. It is like He recycles the bad and turns it around to benefit His children. So, even in the hardest of times, I know He is going to make this work out for me. This is why I can be grateful even for the hard days I have gone through.

Plus, until you have actually walked the path, you can only give one dimensional directions to others. For me to tell you how to get somewhere I have never been, I'd have to Google Map it. I could then tell you to go left for five miles, then go right on Main

Street, but there would be no way for me to tell you what the route smells like. I have no sense whether the route is safe, a beautiful drive, or if the people along the way are friendly. I don't know to tell you about the quaint café that is between point A and point B with a killer macchiato that you have to try. Because I've never personally been down that road, I can't speak about these things. In the same way, we can only help others to the degree that we have persevered ourselves. So when you're in the midst of your mess, press on , don't park and pout. Once we have gained experience and walked through some stuff, God will use us to a greater degree to help others walk through their junk and into their victories.

Blessed be the God and Father of our Lord Jesus Christ, the Father of mercies and God of all comfort, who comforts us in all our affliction so that we will be able to comfort those who are in any affliction with the comfort with which we ourselves are comforted by God. For just as the sufferings of Christ are ours in abundance, so also our comfort is abundant through Christ.

2 Corinthians 3-5 (NASB)

Seasons change soon enough without us having to wish them away. It seems in summer we long for a cool fall breeze. In fall, we dream of the holidays and the sparkle they bring. Once winter sets in, we beg for a spring bloom to awaken the naked branches. In spring we say, "Oh, when will it be warm enough to swim?"

I think contentment is less about gratefully staying in the season you are in, and more about trusting a good God who is faithful to change the season at the right time, every time. If we trust God, we must trust His timing as well.

The fruit from applying these practices may take longer to grow than you anticipate. It is in these times that you must remember, God is so good and always has your best interest in mind.

We must remind ourselves to be grateful, not just because God is working things together for our good, but also because we are called according to His purpose. Our focus must not be on the temporal but on the eternal. The thing about temporary things is, well, they are temporary. I know, super deep insight. You're welcome. Really think about it though. It is human nature to base the majority of our happiness and sadness on fleeting things, things that don't last. I mean, really, how dumb is that? Not to offend you, dear sir or madam, but if your happiness is hinged on things that don't last longer than a vapor, you have entered complete foolery.

No matter what, we can be grateful and content, just like Paul. In whatever state we are in, we can be grateful. How can we do this? Put our focus on eternal things and trust that God is working on our behalf, even when temporary things totally stink, and stuff is hitting the fan like crazy. God remains faithful. He is faithful to pull you out of financial wreckage. However, He is so big, smart, and wise, He multi-purposes His rescue. Not only will He save you financially, but He will use you to help others. Now that right there is something to fuel your gratitude tank for years to come!

This is the day that the Lord has made. We will rejoice and be glad in it.

Psalm 118:24 (NKJV)

Take a moment to reflect on these questions:

Where is your focus right now? Is it on self or others?

Take a moment to think about the blessings you have in your life during this season.

What have you walked through that has made you better off than you were before?

God, we are so grateful for who you are. From each breath we breathe, to the miracle of salvation, you have been generous and kind to us. Lord, help us to frame each situation within your character and love for us. We know you will turn everything around to benefit those who love you. Thank you. Amen.

FOCUS ON YOUR STRENGTHS; CONTRACT YOUR WEAKNESSES

"What if the reason you don't know what you are called to do is you that you are called to do something no one has ever done before?"

— LISA BEVERE

In this chapter lies one of my favorite secrets to wealth and happiness. I am telling you, you will thank me with all of the thank you notes when you begin to get this. And I beg you, please, really get this. Focusing on your strengths and contracting your weaknesses is more than a simple action step. It must be a shift in mentality as well as a lifestyle. This key difference separates the boys from the men here, folks. This is the difference between mom and pop and the big time. This is Branson vs. Hollywood. (We love you Branson, but you're no Hollywood.) This mentality will free you forever in each arena of your life, if you will let it. As a husband, wife, father, mom, career person, or homemaker, each area can be adjusted by truly digesting and developing this one, simple principle.

The Creator has purposefully made us unique. It is what He does. He sees eternity as a whole. He watches the parade from the bird's eye view. He knows right at what time and place a gift is needed within people to complete the tasks at hand. He skillfully crafted us according to His purposes, which are higher than our purposes. When He made you, He had eternity in mind. In creating you, He even had other people's eternities in mind. He placed within you seeds to help change someone else's eternal destination. Wow, really let that meld a minute. Within you lies the potential to make a difference in whether someone spends forever in heaven or in hell.

How amazing is it that God would create us to have so much impact? Flaws and all, He uses us. Strengths He has deposited within us are let out to draw others to His love. However, it is when we try to fit into everyone else's mold that we lose. We all lose. We become vanilla, beige, and monotone. Our voice is silenced, and our impact is minimal. I can relate to wanting to blend in more. How many times have I felt like a fish out of water at a ladies conference? Each lady seems to be bathed in bedazzled glory from head to toe, while I sport my ripped jeans, heels, and t-shirt. Wait, she is the preacher? Yes, yes, it's me. The rag-a-muffin back here, I am the preacher.

The things that make you unique, as well as the things you are naturally gifted in, are your strengths. There is great flavor and life when we all bring exactly who we are to the table. Why are grown-butt people still walking around seeking other people's approval like pubescent middle schoolers? I will tell you why. It is because we have criticized each other with little or no grace, for so long causing fear to be our behavioral compass. We fear being misheard, fear being misunderstood, fear making a mistake, fear not being liked. I am ready for this next generation of believers to be so solid in their faith and standing with Jesus that they live to only please Him and nobody else. Together we are better, but baby, if you can't handle me the way God made me, I will have to be "together" with someone else.

There is nothing better than coming alive doing what you were created to do, along side the people you were created to do it with. On the contrary, there is nothing more defeating than feeling that there is no venue for you to be the person you were made to be, nor are there people to do it with. There was a season in my life when I was surrounded by people with whom I seemed to just not mesh. I liked them; I think they might have liked me, though I can't say for sure. One thing I know is I just didn't click with this group. Before I would text an individual in the group, I would reread the text at least ten times. I would question my wording and how they might interpret it. My motives and intentions seemed to always be put to the test. Nothing was easy or flowed with them. It felt like running in waist-high water. Dialogue felt lethargic and draining. I was miserable having to constantly prove my worth. Friends, this is not how it is supposed to be. Relationships weren't meant to make you feel trapped in an air-tight box labeled "Normal."

However, have you ever been in an atmosphere where you instantaneously felt at home, or met someone you clicked with right away? (Like, belly laugh, can't breathe types of connections.) You felt valued, appreciated, and especially wanted. This is the heart of God, that we all find a family in which we belong! If we aren't careful, we will spend too much time trying to change in order to thrive in an atmosphere we were never meant to occupy in the first place.

Read almost any leadership book and it will tell you that energy invested in strengthening weakness bears little return. On the other hand, it only takes a small amount of energy invested in fine tuning your strengths to profit maximum return. If we aren't careful, we will weaken the seed of potential God has deposited within us just by trying to dilute and balance something within us we were never meant to dilute and balance.

My husband is a most persuasive salesman and marketing guru. It is just who he is. He breathes branding and market infiltration. The man can talk me into anything, and trust me, he has. I mean, we were engaged after meeting only twice. True story. (However, as far as my kids know, we knew each other two years and it was an arranged marriage by our parents.) Actually, he can talk anyone into anything. He describes things with such an energy that you want to be a part of whatever he is talking about. He is very convincing. This is just who Steven is. He is Mr. Sales. It takes little effort from him to sell. However, do not ask the man to keep up with the bills, do inventory or design a logo. This wears on him and drains his energy. He has learned not to waste his time or energy on the things he is not naturally good at. He doesn't try to be good at balancing the books, managing the projects or even craftsmanship. He just does what *he* does. He sells. He markets. He networks.

One thing Steven and I noticed was that whenever we focused on doing what only we could do, people began to take notice. Why? Because we became better and better at what we did well, not just less rank at what we were bad at to start. At the end of the day, it is what you do better than others that makes you more valuable. As you focus on building your strengths, the margin between you and the average bear widens, and one day, you wake up and people are calling you the expert in your field.

Take a deep breath. This is always a process. I have been where you are, and I know what you are thinking. "Must be nice to have everyone else do what you don't want to, but I can't afford that." Listen. There have been seasons when we have done everything. However, slowly and surely, we would work ourselves out of the tasks that we were no good at.

Seek out those who are strong where you lack. Things you loathe doing, others love doing. Let them fill in the voids while you focus on building your money spot. Begin to write down the things you do not like doing, that you don't want to do or that you are not good at. I guarantee you, there are people who specialize in every one of those areas. Not only that, it is probably more affordable to employ their services than you think. Research the costs of these services. Now you have a monetary goal to be able to slowly work yourself out of your weaknesses.

As you leverage more time to strengthening your natural talents, you will become more valuable as the expert in your field. How much time have you already wasted trying to strengthen your weakness, only to find that you are still weak, just maybe not quite as terrible? Quit wasting your time, energy, and resources on your weaknesses! Instead, invest them into your strengths. Build your gifts. Build your gifts. Build your gifts. A thousand times I say, "Build your gifts!" Put all of your energy, all of your thoughts, all of your passion, all of your work, all of your time, and all of your research into building *your* gifts. This is where you will find freedom. It is what you are exceptionally good at that makes you valuable to others. You don't make money by being a jack of all trades. There are no awards for being Mr. or Mrs. Balance. There is no crown and nobody will being handing you roses while telling you to walk the stage for your exceptional ability to be okay at everything. So, why have so many made this their goal?

Give yourself permission to not be good at what you are not good at. For instance, it is okay if I have chronic "can't organize my way out of a paper sack" syndrome. I am okay with being horrible at details. It is fine that I never remember where I put some stuff, all the stuff, actually. However, it is only fine because I have learned to stay in my lane. I will write the words and speak the words, while others decorate the stuff and organize the systems. Words are my home. Communicating is my air. Writing and speaking effortlessly awakens a part of me that nothing else can. It is who I am, and it is what I do. Organizing details and crafty décor-type stuff? Not so much.

So, dear reader, be free to be the you you were made to be. This is where the deep breath of who you are supposed to be can breathe again. No longer be confounded by unrealistic expectations to be good at it all. Instead, you just be you. You are good at being you, great even. So be you, and be the best dang you that you can be. In this slice of eternity, we must do what God made us to do. When we are driving in our own lane, we are able to supply to the body of Christ, what we were meant to supply. As we add our unique ingredient, the body is built up and grows.

(Christ) from whom the whole body, being fitted and held together by what every joint supplies, according to the proper working of each individual part, causes the growth of the body for the building up of itself in love.

Ephesians 4:16 (NASB)

What is your supply? The body of Christ grows at the same ratio to which each part is properly working. I pray that you would own what God has supplied you with and function in the way He has made you. Yes, it is a business principle that you will become more valuable as you sow into your giftings. Yes, it is a natural evolution that you will make more money as the margin between your talents and those of others widens. However, the truth is, the body of Christ will grow in strength and in reaching souls the more we function how we were called to function. Hear the call of eternity, my friend. You were made for a purpose. Lean into it.

Take a moment to reflect on your strengths and weaknesses:

Think of three of your strengths.

Now think of one thing you can do to help grow each strength.

What is one area you would like never to have to work in again?

Is there a company that supplies this service?

If yes, call and get an estimate on how much this service would cost. Write down that amount, and you will have a financial amount you can believe God for.

Father, I ask that you would show me my strengths. Guide me on how I can give myself fully to my gifts and optimize on who you have made me to be. Help me to boldly embrace all you have placed within me. Lord, I ask that you would connect me with the right people for this season. Amen.

FIND AND CONNECT WITH FINANCIAL MENTORS AND COLLEAGUES

"You are the average of the five people you spend the most time with."

— JIM ROHN

Without counsel purposes are disappointed: but in the multitude of counselors they are established.

Proverbs 15:22 (KJV)

The thing about perspective is it can change depending on your vantage point. Someone who is seated higher or has gone down a path further, will have insight for someone earlier in his journey. This is why it is so important to gather successful people around you. Some may be alongside of you in this journey, some up ahead and further along. Either way, the value of adding successful mentors and colleagues is priceless.

Mentors can show you what you do not see or did not even know was possible. They can stretch you to do more, to go further. A mentor can tell you, "Hey, I know this seems impossible, but you can do this."

He who walks with wise men will be wise, but the companion of fools will suffer harm.

Proverbs 13:20 (NASB)

I am thinking of two couples in particular from whom we financially glean. Both couples are radically and irrationally generous. They chose to make Jesus Lord of their money, and because of this, I cannot even begin to tell you the lives and souls that have been impacted. They have taught us that there is no lid when it comes to giving. Just when you think you can't give another dime, one conversation with one of these folks will challenge your faith to believe God for more. They have deposited within us such an eternal perspective as we've heard them talk, tell their stories. We have also been on the receiving end of their generosity, and know it personally. Their faith in God's ability to meet every need and give every good gift as well as their love for every soul is contagious. Their love is loud, like really loud. Like, "Jones', get your butt in the game; you're just in the warm-up!" loud. Just hanging around these couples makes us feel like we can do more, be more, give more, grow more, and God will use us more.

Honestly, this practice is one of the most important ones. We would have hit a plateau years ago had we not pursued such relationships. We have been exposed to such great depths of wisdom in business practices and God practices. If you are the biggest giver you know, you will create a lid of how far your reach can be. Our eyes are constantly widened to the possibilities of our finances whenever we are around people who give more than we do.

We have another couple mentor who has given us the most valuable tools, just by telling us their story. Listening to how the redemptive hand of God has worked on their behalf over the decades has relieved the stress of thinking we have to do everything right. They have taught us of God's grace in marriage when things get tough. We have heard how even through their personal difficult seasons, God was faithful. If He was faithful for them, then we know He will be for us too. They have been such a useful resource for freedom from added mental strains, business pressure, anxiety and stress and for this, we are grateful.

Couples who are transparent, open, and honest about the victories as well as the struggles have really been a secret weapon for us. We feel prepared to handle the highs and the lows. Those who have been real life evidence of God's goodness right before our eyes have helped teach us how to handle situaitions. Again, if God did it for them, we can know that He will do it for us (and you too).

For God does not show favoritism.
Romans 2:11 (NIV)

Surrounding yourself with valuable mentors is easier than you think. First, you must rid yourself of the preconceived ideas you have about the mentor/mentee relationship. I used to think that to be a true mentor, someone would need to sit with me for about an hour a week. They would give me reading assignments, assess my growth, and allot time for me to ask questions. Although part of me would love, and almost even craves this, the reality is, most people are not willing or able to set aside such a big chunk of dedicated time on a reoccurring basis. So, I say, we redefine our win for a mentor. We see our mentors about every other month. We don't drill them with questions or put pressure on them to say something amazing. We take them to dinner (yes, we pay), and we casually cultivate conversations from which we can learn. We have found if we value people and their insight, an organic relationship will develop. Thank God.

I am telling you, this is a make or break practice right here. If you don't already have a relationship with someone you can learn from financially, find someone! You may have to look for a while. There may be some hits and misses. Keep going; keep trying; keep searching; and once you find these people, honor them. Knock until a door is open. Trust me when I tell you that this relationship is so crucial to your success that it is worth your humility. If you get a "no," ask someone else. Don't ask them for a whole evening at first or even for coffee. Ask for five minutes of their time. Show up where it is most convenient for them, and then stick to the five minutes. Come prepared to connect. Ask questions and be clear. Next month, ask for 15 minutes. Work up to a coffee date. Then, watch as the relationship unfolds naturally.

If people know you value their time and you will honor the moments they have set aside for you, they will trust you to give you more. Here is a free little tip for you. The next time you are around a financial mentor, remember this. It may have been a while since someone paid for something for them, so buy their meal or pay for their coffee. A two dollar coffee can go a long way in the heart of someone who often feels the obligation to pick up the tab. If I may be quite frank, people who have money often feel taken advantage of. You have never seen twenty chatty people get so quiet at a restaurant table while the server comes with the bill when they know a wealthy person is among them.

If you own a business, you know friends are always wanting hand-outs. If you make your living off of consulting, you know people are always pilfering advice. To cultivate a healthy mentor relationship, look to give back as much as your mentors are putting in. This will honor them as well as make the whole process enjoyable for them. They'll soon be asking when you can meet again!

I think I have made it very clear that mentors are quite the valuable asset. There is a powerful relationship safety net when you can cultivate both mentors and colleagues. Be sure not to negate those on your same success plane. A mentor can relate to you by where they have been. A colleague can relate to you by where they currently are. Strategies and struggles are freshest when shared by someone who is right where you are, thinking all of your thoughts and feeling all of your feels. Having similar struggles creates a trust and comfort level in which you can freely communicate. Within this type of community, we have found freedom to speak openly and honestly.

To be honest with you, as we climbed the economic ladder, I never imagined our friendships would change as much as they did. We had a great core group of people in our friendship circles. Just as normal friends do, we celebrated victories together and collaborated together on what to do about struggles. Unfortunately, slowly, unbeknownst to us as our financial status raised, we were slowly growing less relatable to our closest friends. Our stresses now looked differently than their stresses. The pressures we had, they didn't have; while things that squeezed them, were non-issues for us. I still remember the sting we felt when we realized this.

One couple in particular comes to mind. This man and woman were our true buds. They were fun, smart, and loved Jesus, but they had declined our invitation to get together for the third time. It was becoming obvious something wasn't peachy in Friendshipville. My husband came right out and asked the other husband what was up. He simply asked, "Hey, I have noticed you guys backing away from us. Did we do something to offend you?" Our friend took a deep breath and began to share transparently what it had been like to be our friends.

They were frustrated and felt like they couldn't keep up. Without thinking, we would casually say, "Let's go here for the weekend. Let's go here to eat. Let's do this, go here, get these!" Like most people, this couple was focused on paying off debt, not taking a weekend get-away. They weren't at a place financially where they could casually do the same things we could. These people were golden and were truly happy for us, but a tension developed as the economic gap widened between friends. They were frustrated because they couldn't afford to do the things we wanted to do together. We were frustrated because we felt that they couldn't understand the pressures of managing, maintaining, and growing like we were. I am glad to say our friendship is still intact, it just looks different now. We have a new normal with them, and that is okay.

We have friends from literally every economic strata. I value each of them. I learn from each of them in different areas. For my friends who are still trying to figure their finances out, we simply don't have the same vantage point. Please hear me. I am in no way discounting the value they add to my life. However, our financial situations just don't relate to one another, and this is fine. I haven't dismissed their influence, I just limit their influence in my life to certain areas. They are not the ones I talk to about financial victories, questions, or struggles, but there are plenty of other areas we commune over. I wouldn't trade these friendships for anything. They mean the world to me. Maybe I don't ask them where I should invest my latest stash, but they are the experts on godly parenting, exercise, church growth, marital relations, and a number of other things.

Evolving friendships on your same economic success level is actually easier than you think. We have found that the higher we go on the ladder, the lonelier the people seem to be. What a trap of the enemy. The enemy wants us to crawl into an elitist corner and become self-centered, counting our cash and licking our "nobody understands me" wounds. May it never be. May we fight even harder for Godly friends the further we go.

Iron sharpens iron; so a man sharpens a friend's character.
Proverbs 27:17 (ISV)

We need each other. If you take these practices and apply them to your life, you will begin to grow financially. It is scriptural, there is no way not to succeed. I urge you to find, cultivate, and invest in friends who are steps ahead of you as mentors, and find those who will walk beside you as colleagues. Ask God to bring the right people for each season. I know He wants to, and I know He will.

Finding a mentor is not as hard as it may seem. Take a moment to reflect on the following questions:

Do you have any financial mentors as of right now?

Can you think of anyone you would like to mentor you?

Write a quick practice email to this desired mentor on the lines provided. Remember to keep it short. Ask for a small amount of time and offer to meet where it is convenient for them.

Do you have any colleagues who are around the same financial status as you who are also on a journey to better themselves monetarily? Name them and a way you can contact them this week.

Lord, I ask that I would recognize when you place a potential mentor or friend in my life. Help me to grow new relationships, as well as cultivate the ones I already have. Lord, let me be aware and available for the right people. Amen

CONCLUSION

Getting rich isn't hard. These gospel centered practices are simple, timeless, and attainable. Attaining wealth God's way dissolves boundaries that try to hinder one's financial success. There is no culture too poor, no village too remote that these principles won't succeed there. When you base your life on words that are alive themselves, there is no doubt that a force stronger than you is at work.

As you work out these principles, all founded in Scripture, there is no doubt that there will be action in the spiritual realm. You will no longer be trying to attain wealth alone, but with the most Mighty One. Continue to yield your ways to His system. Working with His currency plan will propel you faster than you think. My prayer is that everyone who reads this book would have their eyes enlightened to the true value of wealth. I pray that your desire to attain financial success would be led by your longing to see people fall in love with Jesus. May your prosperity be partnered with His purpose.

When our heart's focus is the same as God's heart, He knows that He can trust us with His wealth. For God's true riches are people, His children. He longs to spend eternity with all of us. This is why we must get rich! This is why we must seek first His way of doing things. We must reach people. Drive your cars; sail your boats; build your houses; but never at the sake of touching people for eternity. God has set up a system to attain wealth, placed it in your hands, and graced you to succeed. The heartbeat of the Father is to be united with His children through the saving grace of Jesus Christ. As long as your goal is to honor Him with your wealth, He will see to it that you remain in His wealth.

I pray as you close this book you will feel closer to attaining wealth than you ever have before. Write these practices down; study them; and incorporate them into your daily living.

"For my thoughts are not your thoughts, neither are your ways my ways," declares the Lord. "As the heavens are higher than the earth, so are my ways higher than your ways and my thoughts than your thoughts. As the rain and the snow come down from heaven, and do not return to it without watering the earth and making it bud and flourish, so that it yields seed for the sower and bread for the eater, so is my word that goes out from my mouth: It will not return to me empty, but will accomplish what I desire and achieve the purpose for which I sent it. You will go out in joy and be led forth in peace; the mountains and hills will burst into song before you, and all the trees of the field will clap their hands. Instead of the thornbush will grow the juniper, and instead of briers the myrtle will grow. This will be for the Lord's renown, for an everlasting sign, that will endure forever."

Isaiah 55:8-13 (NIV)

I close out this guide to your new journey with encouragement. I know you can do this! You have got this, dear reader! And God has got you! Since these are practices founded upon the one true Word of God, they cannot return void. These words have been sent to you for you to take them, apply them, and let God fulfill His purpose, as only He can. We must do our part, but rest assured, the part He is doing is much bigger. He is working behind the scenes at a steady pace to see wealth come to you on time, at the right time. He is planting in you good things! As His heart is to increase you, may yours be to increase others. Be diligent to keep walking, but let Him be the one to split the sea. Trust that He is doing a whole lot more than you can see at the moment, and keep swinging.

ABOUT THE AUTHOR

Jamie Jones is an author, preacher, and Christian leader. She has been married to her business guru husband for over 11 years, and has two amazing children, Raleigh, 7 and Ryder, 6. The family has recently embraced it's newest member, Jonesy Gun Jones, the world's coolest Goldendoodle.

Jamie was raised in small town Texas. She was saved at an early age and has been in full-time ministry since she was 21. Her mission is to impart an eternal mindset in all of those she reaches. Her message boasts of God's handiwork in each person He has crafted. Therefore, she longs to empower the body of Christ with bravery and a hunger to authentically be themselves.

Jamie loves to travels and speak to all types of groups. She has a straightforward, humorous approach to teaching that captivates audiences both young and old, male and female. Jamie's creative approach to pulpit ministry is most beneficial in church services, ladies' meetings, leadership training, and youth events.

To book Jamie, go to **jamiejones.org**.

No Strings Attached

NO STRINGS ATTACHED IS AN OUTREACH OF JAMIE JONES MINISTRIES TO LOCAL STRIP CLUBS. IT STARTED WHEN JAMIE HAD A BURDEN TO PRAY AND TO GO TO THOSE IN THE COMMERCIAL SEX INDUSTRY. SO SHE GATHERED 5 OF HER CRAZIEST FRIENDS AND SAID, "LET'S REACH STRIPPERS FOR JESUS!".

ONCE A MONTH A GROWING TEAM OF VOLUNTEERS GATHERS TO ASSEMBLE GIFTS AND PRAY FOR THE DANCERS. A SMALL GROUP THEN DELIVERS THE GIFTS TO THE STRIP CLUBS. THE GOAL IS TO BUILD RELATIONSHIPS WITH THE WOMEN AND LET THEM KNOW THAT JESUS LOVES THEM JUST HOW THEY ARE. AS YOU CAN IMAGINE, BEING IN THE COMMERCIAL SEX INDUSTRY CAN TAKE TOLL ON YOUR SOUL. THEY ARE DOUBTFUL THAT A GOOD GOD LOVES THEM, SKEPTICAL HE COULD EVER WANT TO BE CLOSE TO THEM AND THINK THEIR FUTURE HOLDS NO HOPE.

MARK 2:17
ON HEARING THIS, JESUS SAID TO THEM, "IT IS NOT THE HEALTHY WHO NEED A DOCTOR, BUT THE SICK. I HAVE NOT COME TO CALL THE RIGHTEOUS, BUT SINNERS."

AS THE GIFTS ARE GIVEN, HOPE OF MORE IS DEPOSITED INTO EACH OF THEIR HEARTS. YOU ARE INVITED TO BE A PART OF THIS JESUS MOVEMENT. THE TWO WAYS TO HELP ARE TO PRAY AND TO GIVE TOWARDS THE GIFTS. FOR MORE INFORMATION, AND UPDATES ON THE OUTREACH, GO TO JAMIEJONES.ORG/NSA.

TO CONNECT WITH

VISIT JAMIEJONES.ORG

- BLOG
- ITINERARY
- CONTACT
- MEDIA

PRAYER OF SALVATION

God loves you — no matter who you are, no matter what your past. God loves you so much that He gave His one and only begotten Son for you. The Bible tells us that "…whoever believes in Him shall not perish but have eternal life" (John 3:16 NIV). Jesus laid down His life and rose again so that we could spend eternity with Him in heaven and experience His absolute best on earth. If you would like to receive Jesus into your life, say the following prayer out loud and mean it from your heart.

Heavenly Father, I come to You admitting that I am a sinner. Right now, I choose to turn away from sin, and I ask You to cleanse me of all unrighteousness. I believe that Your Son, Jesus, died on the cross to take away my sins. I also believe that He rose again from the dead so that I might be forgiven of my sins and made righteous through faith in Him. I call upon the name of Jesus Christ to be the Savior and Lord of my life. Jesus, I choose to follow You and ask that You fill me with the power of the Holy Spirit. I declare that right now I am a child of God. I am free from sin and full of the righteousness of God. I am saved in Jesus' name. Amen.

If you prayed this prayer to receive Jesus Christ as your Savior for the first time, please contact us on the Web at **www.harrisonhouse.com** to receive a free book.

Or you may write to us at

Harrison House • P.O. Box 35035 • Tulsa, Oklahoma 74153

The Harrison House Vision

Proclaiming the truth and the power
Of the Gospel of Jesus Christ
With excellence;

Challenging Christians to
Live victoriously,
Grow spiritually,
Know God intimately.